MISSION ACAPULCO

This book is a rewarding read that tells the story of how Jay's persevering faith and his apostolic-like ministry through Mission Acapulco in Mexico unexpectedly came into being. It will also help the reader to see how the Lord may stir up and energize spiritual gifts of service in anyone, no matter how old or what stage of life they happen to be in. Jay's narration of his own journey of faith and discovery will be helpful to all believers seeking to know how they might serve God better or more abundantly.

- **Bruce Quinlan,** DMin, MDiv, MBA, MA, MA, CPA, RMHCI

Jay's journey to Acapulco, Mexico is a reminder to anyone who thinks their spiritual race is over. It's never too late to conquer mountains, spread the gospel, and live out the purposes of God. Jay unfolds story after story of God's grace, miracle working power, and deliverance. God can use anyone and Jay has shown how obedience will always open the door for God's Kingdom to advance.

- **Larry Burgbacher,** Faith Church

MISSION ACAPULCO

THE ROCKY ROAD OF A MISSIONARY TO MEXICO

BY JAY DE VRIES

The events, locations, and conversations are as the author remembered them. This work allows for discrepancies in the translation of the author's notes, however it remains true to the persons, locations, and circumstances.
This is a factual representation based on the best recollection of the author.

Copyright © 2021 Jay De Vries

All rights reserved. No part of this publication may be reproduced, distributed, or transmitted in any form or by any means, including photocopying, recording, or other electronic or mechanical methods, without the prior written permission of the publisher, except in the case of brief quotations embodied in critical reviews and certain other noncommercial uses permitted by copyright law. For permission requests, write to the publisher, addressed "Attention: Permissions Coordinator," at the address below.

Paperback: 978-1-951475-16-1
Ebook: 978-1-951475-17-8

Library of Congress Control Number: 2021905458

First paperback edition: May 2021

Edited by Scott Massey
Cover Art by Keana Reyes

Arrow Press Publishing
Summerville, SC 29486

www.arrowpresspublishing.com

CONTENTS

Editor's preface	1
Acknowledgments	3
A Disturbing Night	6
Meeting Jenny & Saul	11
City By The Bay Of Reeds	15
The Call Of An Elderly Sea Captain	18
Captain Brenton's Legacy	21
Triumphant Arrival	25
Encounter With A Drug Dealer	29
All Is Not Well	32
Miracle Of The Resurrected Truck	38
Meeting Sammy & Pamela	41
Miracle Of The Flat Tire	46
Emails From God	49
Unselfing	55
Stripped Of Religion	60
Sammy & Pamela	71
Quiet Tears	77
The Proclaimer	83
Following God's Direction	86
Palenque	90
Like A Scene From The Book Of Acts	96
Church In A Rock	103
Time To Leave	107
Thoughts On The Bus	110

First Trip Back: Heal The Sick, Cast Out Devils	113
Another Return Trip: Back To The Mountains	119
Third Trip Back: Leadership Training	124
Foot Washing: Leadership Training Part II	133
Looking For Joshua	139
References	146

EDITOR'S PREFACE

This book should have been published sooner. For that, I apologize. First, I don't think I was quite prepared for the amount of work involved in transposing someone else's thoughts and words into a readable format.

Then there were the unexpected life events like an emergency renovation caused by water leaks, our daughter's declining health due to Crohn's requiring another renovation so she and our granddaughter could move back in with us, the COVID pandemic (though in actuality, that was a blessing as it gave me time to write due to restaurant dining room closures).

I think the hardest obstacle to overcome was myself. My self-doubts and feelings of unworthiness for such a project; my struggles with procrastination and my own sins. Depression. But as I worked on each chapter Jay dumped in my lap (at times that was how I felt), I saw my struggles mirrored with Jay's. During this entire process, Jay patiently waited. He never chided me for being slow, he only encouraged.

Editor's Preface

I met Jay at Pointe North Community Church in Moncks Corner, SC around 2011. At that time, I felt the Lord tell me to make Jay my mentor. I was struggling with trust issues and had no idea how to make that happen. Then Jay asked me to be part of a team to go to Mexico. Through prayer and testing, I found no way to go, finances being a major setback; though I felt in my heart I really should go.

I had another opportunity in late 2012 when Jay was organizing a small group to go with him to Acapulco in the summer of 2013. I determined to go this time and the Lord provided. The events of that trip with only five others from Pointe North showed me that God was working in Southwest Mexico: reading Captain Brenton's Bible notes; meeting Sammy and Pamela and seeing the enthusiasm and love for Jesus in them and the group of young people they led; two lines that the Lord gave me for a poem I wrote for Acapulco several months before the trip that turned out to be the exact words the Lord spoke to Sammy to encourage him; the conversion of an entire village of young people just by playing soccer.

God is working in Acapulco. He is using broken and dirty vessels, that He is cleaning and repairing for the work. It is His work.

I'm sorry it took so long to get this done, but I suspect the Lord was aware when He handed me this assignment. I hope Jay's telling of his part in this work in Southwest Mexico encourages and inspires you.

- **Scott D. Massey**

ACKNOWLEDGMENTS

God supplies specific people at each phase of the work. There are far too many to mention that there are certain ones in each segment that were used in a powerful way in this journey.

The first two years: Vicki Vasquez, as well as her son Victor helping with translating and teaching me basic Spanish. A bit later Mauricio Corona and his wife Linda were great mentors, friends, and ministry partners. I also have to mention David Monterey as well as Ricardo Mojica. And it goes without saying that Sammy and Pamela Morales who are now the directors and pastors of the main church probably helped me much more than I helped them.

I need to thank all the board members who over the years supplied funding. I did not take a salary or any money in Mexico. All the money raised went to pay the Spanish pastors and helpers as well as buy food and supplies for the churches. I cannot name them all but only a couple that were with the cause right from the start. Our heartfelt thanks to Bruce Perdue who has never left in his unwavering support and encouragement for this ministry. I also need to remember Scott Benedict, Jon Summers, Larry Marino, Scott Benedict, Randall Poindexter, Ron Alber, and Lorne Shumack, as well as Jim Muckenfuss who made the first exploratory trip with me to Mexico. There are many others that served on committees, fundraising, as well as short terms on the Board of Directors for which I am so deeply indebted.

CHAPTER 1
A DISTURBING NIGHT

I woke up in a panic. It felt like a hand was pinning me down, like I was tied, face down, to the poorly built bed I found myself in. I had piled three thin mattresses on the slat boards and I could now feel each board against my ribs. My pillow was soaked. Blood? The only sound in this cold dark room somewhere in the border town of Nuevo Laredo, Mexico was this old man weeping like a baby—and I couldn't stop.

And I was speaking. I was listing all that I had bought to secure my American dream retirement. Each item inventoried, its place of purchase, its cost to the penny. My double wide mobile home, complete with fireplace and jacuzzi. My deck and workshop built by my hands. My truck and my four-wheeler. My boats and pontoon. My travel trailer. A new bicycle. More furniture and televisions than any one old man needed. My 40-plus rods & reels. Four new rifles. Two pistols. Shotguns for skeet, dove, duck, quail —over 25. Sportsmen's clothing, hats, and boots.

A Disturbing Night

Shame covered me like the shabby quilts I used to fend off the cold. The last hours of the night I continued to break out in tears, occasionally feeling peace, but always afraid and confused. "Why am I here? Why...am...I...here?"

Most of my life had been spent faking piety performing formalities, participating in false spirituality, building a religion around my goals and my accomplishments. I went to schools in Michigan and Florida and acquired degrees. I was the director of a ministry in Holland, MI while continuing advanced studies in psychology. I built chapels and counseled heroin addicts. Eventually, I wanted to become financially independent; I didn't want to rely on wages from the church of any denomination. Self-sufficiency became my goal and the insurance industry my means. And I was very successful. My wife and I moved about Ohio and finally settled in Charleston, SC with our four children and twin boys we took in.

Then my ideal life was blown about like a bag of garbage in a hurricane—literally. In the fall of 1989 Hurricane Hugo swept through South Carolina wreaking havoc up through the state. Due to the tremendous loss, I was forced to sell my agency. Eventually, my wife and I separated. These were hard times for me.

I continued in insurance and eventually retired at the ripe old age of 66. I moved to the rural area of Pineville and began to settle into my well-deserved retirement. I bought a pontoon boat to lure my grown children over, hoping to build better relationships with them, to spend time with them. I started a charter fishing business and captained boats to justify my love of fishing. And I became active in three area churches thinking that that would be sufficient to scratch a spiritual itch. But God wanted more. So much more.

I became involved in the community organizing street cleanups, neighborhood watch programs, and teaching Bible studies at a small church in the area. Because the distance to my home church, Cathedral of Praise, was now greater, I became a member of a large church in Moncks Corner, Pointe North Community Church, which was much closer.

One of my great joys was to relax on the front or back porch. At night, deer would walk through the front yard as I sat, as well as rabbits and an occasional possum; in the early morning wild turkey would gather in the back yard. But after a year of living my American dream, a very heavy sense of boredom overtook me while sitting on that porch one evening. Within a couple of days the joy of my lifestyle was completely gone.

I tried to make changes in my life by doing more things in church, like organizing different ways to help the poor in the community; but nothing relieved me of this boredom bordering on depression.

I spoke to one of the pastors at Pointe North, Steve Stahl. He simply said that maybe God had something else for me. His suggestion was to visit a Bible school in Nuevo Laredo, Mexico for two weeks to see what the Lord may have for me. This sounded like a very crazy idea, but because I was feeling bad enough I agreed to at least contact Mr. Dave, the man who ran the school. After some time of thinking and praying (stalling) about the idea, I finally called—only to get an answering machine. I left my name and number, and honestly, was quite relieved as a couple of weeks passed and I had heard nothing.

And then Mr. Dave called.

I was invited to join a mission group from Oklahoma City in early January to distribute Bibles. Against my better judgment, I agreed to go. At the very least it would give me a break from my boredom and a chance to experience something different. Maybe

A Disturbing Night

when I got back, I would have a greater appreciation for all the good things I had in my possession.

When I arrived in Laredo, Texas Mr. Dave greeted me and immediately took me to the Bible school center, and we loaded his truck with supplies. Crossing the border into Mexico was like entering a different world. Laredo, Texas is a normal American city, the streets are clean and wide with relatively few potholes. Directly across the border, the narrow roads are littered with trash and it seems there are more holes than pavement. Poverty hits you in the face. Houses pieced together of scrap wood, tin sheets, and cardboard lined the broken streets. Even though many of these people work for the Caterpillar plant that had moved from Texas, they only made less than $6.00 a day. You could tell the people who had money, their houses were surrounded by high walls with broken glass embedded in the top to keep others from climbing over.

Arriving at the Bible school in Nuevo Laredo, I found it to be very plain, but functional. Most of it had been built by mission groups. I was to stay in an unfinished dormitory for students. There were two handmade bunk beds with extremely thin mattresses, an old armchair that when sat in your bottom hit the floor, no heating or air conditioning, and the shower was a pipe in the wall. I was assured that there would be warm water for a short period early in the morning.

It had been a long day (I had got up that morning at 3:00 AM to drive to the Charleston airport) and I was ready to rest. Mr. Dave told me there would be an early morning praise & worship service and introductions to the group from Oklahoma arriving later that night. I read a book for a bit, and then, to fulfill my religious duties, I read from the Bible and prayed. I recall that I prayed specifically for God to give me a good attitude while I was here, as my current attitude was quite negative. And I prayed that He would show me if there was something I needed to learn or do, to make it clear to me.

About 10:00 PM I arranged three of the mattresses on the slat boards of one bunk, took two of the quilts from the other beds, and put on two sweaters to fend off the cold. (I was told in the morning that ice had formed in the fountain in front of the school, something that had not happened before.) I had expected the temperature to be warmer than South Carolina, so I had not packed clothes for the cold, and, as I said, there was no heating. I fell asleep still very unsettled about being here and I was already counting down the time when I would leave. Shortly thereafter, I woke up covered in tears thinking it was blood.

CHAPTER 2
MEETING JENNY & SAUL

I seldom have dreams that I remember and have never had a vision, but I had asked God why I was here, and He had clearly responded: You have to change. I lay awake the rest of the night afraid and confused.

I got out of bed around 6:00 and put on as many clothes as I could find. I headed to the kitchen where I saw lights on. I couldn't speak to anyone, as the cooks only knew Spanish; but they understood "coffee". Standing very close to the wood burning stove I warmed up while eating a bowl of oatmeal. By this time some of the folks from Oklahoma City came in. Forcing a smile and trying to be friendly, I thought to myself, "Great. I have to talk to these people." I really wasn't in the mood at that moment for small talk with strangers and I certainly did not say anything about my experience that night.

We all entered the chapel for the morning service, and as there was no heat there either, I found a sunlit bench in the back.

Everyone introduced themselves, there was a short message and some wonderful singing, but I don't remember any of it. My mind was totally confused.

When the service ended, I tried to leave, but a young lady approached me. Speaking English, she introduced herself as Jenny and explained that she was from Oklahoma and had married a Mexican man from the mountain area just north of Acapulco. They had been praying and God told them they needed to talk to me. Now this really aggravated me. I wanted to ask them if God had sent them an e-mail or written them a note. But I had nowhere to go, so I listened and agreed to talk to them more later.

Confusion. Anger. Fear. What did all this mean? I kept it all to myself as we piled onto the bus that would take us to a park in Nuevo Laredo to hand out invitations to hear music, see drama, and receive food. The pot-hole filled road could be seen speeding past through holes in the floor. At some point in the day, I decided to share my experience with the leader of the Bible school, but he didn't seem surprised. He simply told me to keep listening and follow what God may have for me.

Eventually, I got to talk to Jenny and her husband, Saul. From my years of experience in ministry and psychology, I could tell that their marriage was in trouble, but it was also obvious that they both had a passion for the hearts of the people living in the moun-

Meeting Jenny & Saul

tains and the city of Acapulco. After hours of talking and sharing and praying I agreed to meet them in Acapulco in May. Don't ask me why I agreed to this; I'm thinking at this point that at my age this is a crazy idea for God to send me to another country. I'm also thinking that I can't wait to get back to South Carolina.

When I did return to South Carolina, I busied myself with my normal activities. But my mind wandered to Mexico. I thought maybe I could go for just a month and help in some way. I shared my experience with the elders at Pointe North, but they were just as confused as I was. Someone suggested that I take one of the elders with me when I went to Acapulco in May. The first that I asked, Jim Muckenfuss, to my amazement, quickly agreed to go. Meanwhile, my life went on as usual.

CHAPTER 3
CITY BY THE BAY OF REEDS

I once visited Acapulco for a conference during my days in the insurance business. The beautiful beaches of Acapulco have been the playground of celebrity for decades—from the wealthy inhabitants of Mexico City in the '20s to the Rat Pack celebrities of the '50s and '60s to middle class Americans of the '70s. And where the rich come to play, the poor come for pay.

Acapulco is a place of contradiction: travel brochures highlight tourist attractions and the high life—luxurious resort hotels, fine dining, and playboy-style nightlife—all next to newspapers splashed with crime scene-like photos of the murder of the day in living color. Absent from any description of Acapulco are the thrown together shops and roadside diners—pallet and cardboard walls, scrap metal roofs, bare concrete floors; the mounds of trash along outlying city streets; or the impoverished mountain villages surrounding this seaside resort.

City by the Bay of Reeds

The prospect of jobs in this prosperous city lured many to seek its security. Earthquakes in Mexico City drove many more to find shelter by the bay. During the last decades of the 20th century and into the 21st, the population of Acapulco exploded within its borders boasting a population, as of this writing, of between 700,000 and 800,000 souls within an area of less than 50 square miles.

The bay area was originally inhabited for centuries by Olmeca, Mezcala, and Náhuatl (who named it acatl-pol—the place of big reeds). In the 1500s, Spanish invaders took over the natural harbor and Acapulco became an important route of trade (including slaves) to Asia and South America.

As a lucrative port, Acapulco became susceptible to pirates and other marauding enemies. Fuerte San Diego was built on the northern peninsula of the bay to guard against their attacks.

It would now appear that pirates still run rampant. Daily gang related killings put Acapulco near the top of the list of most violent cities in the world, though claims are made that tourists are safe within the resort area. Drug cartels roam the hillsides jealously protecting their turf. Prostitution and sex trafficking thrive.

But God has always had a plan for this bay of bruised reeds.

RELIGION IN GUERRERO

89.2 % CATHOLIC

4.4 % PROTESTANT/EVANGELICAL

2 % OTHER CHRISTIAN

0.1 % JEWISH

0.4 % OTHER

3.1 % NONE

0.9 % NOT SPECIFIED

CHAPTER 4
THE CALL OF AN ELDERLY SEA CAPTAIN

I was amazed at how the city had changed. Many more hotels lined the costera, the beach strip around Acapulco harbor. The noise of unbelievable traffic assaulted our ears. Pollution from the multitude of taxis and busses filled the air. Trash was everywhere. I did not want to live in this.

While waiting for Jenny and Saul to pick us up, Jim and I prayed. "Lord, I need a sign from you. Do I really have to come here?"

Jenny and Saul arrived in a van with no AC that they had driven from Oklahoma. We were looking for a pastor they had not met, who had no idea we were coming; but he was someone who knew the needs of the people in the mountains. We paid a taxi driver who knew where he lived and followed him to the pastor's home.

Houses and shops are connected in Acapulco, except for a few of the very rich. We found the entrance, a little steel door that

The Call of an Elderly Sea Captain

led to a few broken steps going down. We knocked on the first steel gate to our left. A middle-aged man with bright eyes and a ready smile greeted us—Pastor Lacko.

Jenny and Saul introduced us, with Jenny as interpreter, and explained the reason for our visit. Pastor Lacko laid out a map on the ground and showed us the mountain areas where he ministered to several small churches of 6 to 8 people, traveling weekly by taxi and then 4-wheeler or pickup truck from village to village over narrow donkey trails and along cliff edges.

As he explained the condition of the Christian church in the mountains he began to cry. "No tenemos ayuda. Hemos pedido ayuda a gritos." (We have no help. We have cried for help.)

Trying to be a good Christian and put on a show of compassion, I joined him on my knees. As I put my hand on his shoulder, God broke my heart. For the first time in my life I cried real tears for the lost. In the past I had faked speaking in tongues, but now the Holy Spirit truly filled me.

Pastor Lacko suddenly got up and went inside. He returned with a little book. He told us it was about Captain Brenton, a 70-year-old sea captain from England who was on loan to the Mexican navy. Highly decorated by the Mexican government for his service, he retired in Guererro. He bought many donkeys and used them to carry Bibles into the mountains of southern Mexico. Pastor Lacko looked directly at me and said, "You are a 70-year-old sea captain and you have been sent here to help us."

Dumbstruck, I asked Jenny if they had told him anything about me. They assured me that Saul had only seen him a couple of times in the mountains and that he knew nothing of my visit to Mexico. You see, I had just turned 70 and they had no idea that I had a captain's license to justify my boats.

Jim looked at me and said, "I think God just dropped a cement brick on your head."

CHAPTER 5
CAPTAIN BRENTON'S LEGACY

Who was the 70-year-old sea captain Pastor Lacko spoke of? Captain Reginald Corey Brenton (1848-1921) was an admiral of the British Navy. The president of Mexico wanted the best of the best to train cadets in the Mexican Navy, so he sent request to Queen Victoria. She recommended Captain Brenton.

For five years Captain Brenton commanded the training frigate *La Zaragosa* and taught at the naval base in Alcapulco. According to Marguerite Boyce in her book <u>Captain Brenton's Heritage</u>, "He had been promoted to the highest rank of the Mexican Navy and was fondly called the *Father of the Mexican Navy* by the first officers to graduate from the *Zaragos* frigate training."

Acapulco became his home away from Britain and his base of operation for distributing Bibles throughout southwest Mexico. Now at this time, the late 1899s, early 1900s, the railroads only went so far from Mexico City and most other roads throughout the region were no more than donkey trails.

Captain Brenton died of complications from malaria in Ometepec, a village in the foothills of the Sierra Madre del Sur 115 miles east of Acapulco. His Spanish Bible that he used during his time in Ometepec was located in 1940. It was photocopied with notes and prayers handwritten in the margins and titled <u>On This Hill A Man Prayed</u>. The following are some of his prayers for Acapulco and southwest Mexico taken from Marguerite Boyce's book and an actual copy of the photocopied Bible. I have included the verses they were written next to.

<u>Genesis 13:14-15</u>

And the Lord said unto Abram, after that Lot was separated from him, Lift up now thine eyes, and look from the place where thou art northward, and southward, and eastward, and westward: For all the land which thou seest, to thee will I give it, and to thy seed forever.

"Oh Lord Jesus give all this West Coast of Mexico to the Gospel of thy grace."

<u>Book of Haggai</u>

"Lord Jesus we most humbly place the preaching of the Gospel in West Mexico before Thee. Great salvation to many."

<u>Psalm 2:8</u>

Ask of me, and I shall give thee the heathen for thine inheritance, and the uttermost parts of the earth for thy possession.

"Lord Jesus, I do solemnly ask of Thee Southwest Mexico as my heritage."

Matthew 15:32

And, behold, a woman of Canaan came out of the same coasts, and cried unto him, saying, Have mercy on me, O Lord, thou Son of David; my daughter is grievously vexed with a devil.

"My daughter Mexico is grievously tormented. Grant repentance and faith in Thee"

Isaiah 38:6

And I will deliver thee and this city out of the hand of the king of Assyria: and I will defend this city.

"Lord save Acapulco. Dec 22, 1920"

Psalm 73:28

But it is good for me to draw near to God: I have put my trust in the Lord God, that I may declare all thy works.

"Lord Jesus I solemnly place the whole hope of evangelization of West Mexico in Thy hands. Work out all the details."

Ephesians 2:10

For we are His workmanship, created in Christ Jesus for good works, which God prepared beforehand that we should walk in them.

I am certainly no admiral nor a man of high rank, but God's direction is clear. I had only begun to realize that none of this is about me, but all is about His grace, His mercy, His purposes, and His glory.

CHAPTER 6
TRIUMPHANT ARRIVAL

Absolutely convinced of the call to go, I began selling all that I had acquired. At first, it was difficult letting go, but with each item gone, each rod and reel and rifle, the load became lighter. The sale of my truck and boats lifted a great weight. This helped me to get out of debt. What I didn't sell I gave away, which gave me more satisfaction than buying it.

I spent a lot of time sharing the story of God's call and putting together a board to help raise funds and give direction to the work. The first board comprised Jim Muckenfuss, John Moody, Bruce Perdue, Greg Engstrom, and John Rackcliff.

I returned to Mexico in October of that year. For the next month I followed Pastor Lacko into the mountains on roads that were nothing more than donkey trails, ruts perhaps once traveled by Captain Brenton. Everyone was amazed at how well I held up under the heat and the travel and the late hours—including me. I took it as another sign that I was to be there. The others had used this month as a test to see if this old man could take it.

A self-assessment of my gifts of public speaking, teaching, and preaching, as well as my strength of personality and desire to be a leader, signified to me that this was my purpose in Mexico. After all, this strong call coming to me at my age must mean that I was to be one of God's top-tier advisors here in Mexico. But in my desire to use my gifts to change the country, I neglected to ask for His direction and His purpose.

I made arrangements to give myself financial freedom, and quite honestly, clout with the Mexican people. I rented out the house I owned. I sold my agency to a man who paid me a lump sum and then would pay me monthly for the next 18 years. I had my social security. Money would be no problem.

But the tenants totally destroyed the house, costing me thousands. The man who bought my agency ran off to another country and stopped all payments. Social security only goes so far. All this forced me to be utterly dependent upon God for everything.

Finding a place to stay presented another challenge. That first trial month I stayed with Saul and Jenny in their tiny apartment. This would not do as a long-term solution. While I was back in the States making my arrangements for a more permanent stay, they located a few apartments for me to look at upon my return.

And my return was not the grand entrance I expected in my heart. A stalled plane in Atlanta delayed my flight's arrival. By the time we taxied to another gate and I could depart the plane, my flight to Mexico City had left. Next flight out—11:00 that night. When I finally arrived in Mexico City at 3:00 A.M., the airline said they would put me up in a hotel room located at the airport. Not speaking Spanish made it difficult to find. I finally did—at 5:00 in the morning. The flight for Acapulco was scheduled to leave at

Triumphant Arrival

9:00. I had no way to contact Saul. My American cell phone didn't work in Mexico. I foolishly put my computer in my bag and all my luggage had gone ahead of me. I ended up paying a fee to send an email from the hotel. After a couple hours of sleep and a short flight, I arrived in Acapulco to find my suitcase broken into and my computer and other items taken.

"So, Lord, this is my welcome to Mexico!"

Saul and Jenny found a couple of apartments for me to look at in between all that they were doing. They continued the work with Pastor Lacko and had begun making progress near the village where Saul was born, while also teaching at a private school to make extra money.

I was not pleased with the area of the first apartment they took me to. Exhausted from my ordeal I consented to stay the night. Looking out the window of this 500 square foot living space lacking air conditioning, I could see the neighbor's window and open doorway 3 feet away. I dropped into bed sweat-soaked.

The next day we found an upstairs apartment on a quiet, narrow street; clean, but small—two tiny bedrooms and a kitchen with a 2-burner stove, a refrigerator with a bungee cord holding the door, and a table with an uncomfortable bench sofa. Later, I would have to buy an air conditioner (that I would have to leave), get used to carrying 6-gallon jugs of water for drinking, and learn to like cold showers. A 2-foot by 12-foot porch overhanging the street gave me a view of the property 15 feet across the street. But there was also just a short 2 block walk to a mountain path that led along the ocean where I could see whale and their young and hear the surf crashing into the rocks.

Once settled in, I felt my popularity was instantaneous. I was convinced that this is what God wanted me to do in Mexico. I prepared 7-10 messages a week. We drove 2-3 hours to coastal mountain villages to sing and teach, give an altar call, then on to the next. We would meet with 2-4 families in a rented 10x10 hut without windows or a church built of split palm logs or a storefront made of poles covered by a tarp or just in the street. But always hot. I would have difficulty reading my notes as the sweat fell from my face and made the ink run. Each time we would sing and teach, give an altar call, then on to the next.

    I had no idea how deep the ministry to those who came forward to pray—all my preparations went into the teachings and I spent no time learning the language, only what I picked up while being immersed in the culture. Besides, my translators were excellent.

CHAPTER 7
ENCOUNTER WITH A DRUG DEALER

Pastor Lacko and I went to the funeral of a friend's son who had been killed by a local cartel. Apparently, he had picked some marijuana from a nearby field, so the cartel cut his body in pieces and laid them at the door of his mother's home.

The people of the mountains surrounding Acapulco make money by leasing their land to the cartels and raising cattle. If you own 10 or more cows, you are considered wealthy, but the crops belong to the cartels. All of it.

While Pastor Lacko ministered to the family, I decided to take a walk down a shaded trail that seemed to lead to the river. About 100 yards down I came to a richly green field. As the thought entered my mind that this may be marijuana, cold metal pressed the back of my neck and the click of a rifle hammer froze me where I stood.

And then a calmness overcame me. I spoke quite clearly in Spanish that my Spanish was limited.

"Then speak English, old man. I will understand."

He stepped around in front of me and held the rifle barrel against my chest. "What are you doing here, old man?"

I showed him my hands. "I have no gun, please put yours down."

He took a step back and lowered his weapon. We stood staring at each other for a moment that lasted a lifetime.

"Why are you in these mountains? Do you work for the police? The military?"

"I am a missionary here to tell you and all people that Jesus died for you and that you can have new life for all of eternity. I am here with a pastor comforting friends and family at a funeral."

"I know this pastor," he said, "and I know of this funeral. The boy should not have stolen. His death sent a message."

"Christ died to send a message."

Encounter With a Drug Dealer

We spoke for a while longer. I tried to share the love of Jesus with him. The Holy Spirit kept me at peace and gave me words. After about a half hour we stood silent.

"My name is _____. Use my name when you are in these mountains. You will be protected. But do not come through my fields again. I would not want to have to kill you."

"I can assure you it will not happen again."

We turned and walked off in opposite directions. When I got to the road leading back, I paused and thanked God and rededicated my life to serve Him in Mexico. I said nothing of the encounter to Pastor Lacko until sometime later.

CHAPTER 8
ALL IS NOT WELL

We often romanticize the life of the missionary, painting a wondrous picture of the saintly man or woman of God serving and following the call. But my situation was nothing of the sort. Believe me when I tell you the next year was the worst of my life.

I felt I needed to move closer to the areas we were ministering to so with the help of Ron Lavender, a real estate agent, and Vicki Vasquez, a wealthy supporter, we found a place owned by a friend of Vicki. It was in a decent part of town, though by American standards horrid. It was the first floor of three. Bars guarded the windows. The bathroom was so small that your elbows touched both walls while sitting on the toilet. And it had no sink; I had to use the kitchen sink to wash. The furniture was completely uncomfortable, so the folks at Pointe North Church bought me a nice recliner. There was a pool though.

Feelings of loneliness and inadequacy began to overwhelm me. I realized that my role here now was that of taxi driver for Pastor Lacko and the others. This became apparent when he asked to borrow $300 for a car and the invitations to go with them became less and less.

I needed to move again. One of Vicki's condos, a place called Lomis del Mar, became vacant and she let me stay there paying the same rent I had been paying for the previous apartment. This was tremendously generous, as the condo, which had lodged a millionaire at one time, had modern amenities and a huge porch with a rollout awning. Standing on the porch, I could look out over the bay to the Pacific Ocean.

There was a nice pool and a well-equipped weight room. I used the weight room frequently as I wasn't doing anything else. Less and less ministry was accomplished by "God's top-tier advisor". Occasionally, I preached English services at a nearby Presbyterian church, but I continued to struggle with my identity and purpose here in Mexico. I struggled with depression that bordered on clinical. Frustration over learning the language only added more burden to my mind. I hired Vicki's son to help me, but I just couldn't get it.

As a diversion, I would go to the beach and walk, enjoying the beauty of the bay. Eventually, I would come back to pondering my purpose here and get pissed off. So I would return to my beautiful rooms, read and try to study, but loneliness would overtake me (I had only one or two people who spoke English to talk to) and I would think maybe I should just go home.

But I couldn't quit. My ego wouldn't let me. I made sure plenty of people knew the incredible story of how God brought me here and the noble journey I had already taken. I couldn't face returning now.

Yet how could I continue. I felt extremely insufficient for this role, whatever that was. To be sure, we had a mission statement: to come alongside small, struggling Christian groups and assist them with training; to help them grow by giving them the tools and knowledge of evangelistic activities. Was this happening? Was there real fruit? Was Mission Acapulco birthing new churches and were older churches exploding with growth? No. In fact, people God had put in my path began to become disgruntled and leave to do other things. My ego and insufficiency blinded me so that I could not see that everything I had been doing was very much centered around me.

Another part of this attack (because all of this was an attack of the enemy), another form of my feelings of insufficiency was my own sin. As I would try to read and study the Bible, all my sin would be clearly brought to my attention. How could a man who has committed sexual sin in thought and deed be a servant of God? I knew I was a Christian, that I could be forgiven, but how could God use me as a minister or missionary? I was living a lie. If these people knew my intense struggles, they would not accept me.

Strong feelings of guilt bore down on me during times of ministry. I am not the leader, the good and upright man these people think I am when they shake my hand, hug my neck at the end of a program. Returning to my apartment, I would look in the mirror and feel evil for fooling these people. I started spending more and more time alone taking long walks or just sleeping.

From my considerable training in psychology, I could recognize the symptoms of depression and felt I knew how to deal with it. I would get on my knees and confess to God my sin. But my motivation was not so much sorrow for my sin as it was a desire to be rid of the guilt.

It is wonderfully true that God is faithful and just and forgives and removes our guilt, however, it is also required that we confess our sins one to another. Pride would not let me do this. The result was that guilt not confessed turned to shame. The feelings of insufficiency turned to feelings of being ashamed of myself for what I was doing. It became difficult for me to minister. All I could do was take others to places of ministry, sit back and watch.

For two months I was a miserable, unhappy, cynical old cuss exasperating those around me. I withdrew myself to the pool often to sit alone and read. One evening, a man about my age sat reading a Bible. I introduced myself and learned that he was a retired minister from Indiana who had lost his wife a short time ago. He was saddened by the loss and needed time to get away and discover what God would have him do next in the time he had left on earth. We talked for a long time and I was eager to convince him of the great work I had been called to do here. He asked me point blank, "Are you happy with your work?" I hesitated to answer.

"I hear in your story that you are struggling. Whatever you share with me, I will keep in confidentiality."

I found this too incredible and made an excuse to leave. I went back up to my apartment, lay on my bed, and cried.

The next morning, I went back to the pool to make notes for a program that evening. I watched for the man to show up again and he did. He walked directly to me and with a warm smile asked me to forgive him for being so direct and offending me the night before. He told me his story of problems with adultery; how his loving wife forgave him, though he didn't deserve it; how God removed his guilt when he confessed his sin to the leadership of his church. After a time, he was reinstated and served 10 more years with gratitude, feeling undeserving of such grace.

"We serve a God who uses broken people, problem people, to minister in a broken world," he said.

It was like arrows going into my heart, God speaking through him directly to me. I opened up and poured out my soul to this stranger. He took my hand and prayed I would believe God had forgiven me.

"If you feel unforgiven, then you would have to call God a liar. Remember, if you confess your sins, God is faithful and just to forgive."

He suggested I study the leaders of the Bible, the prophets and kings, as well as leaders in the New Testament.

"See who Jesus used. Not the learned, or those who worked hard to keep the law, but those who acknowledged their sin and gave all glory to God. Remember, this is God's work, not yours. Be honest about yourself with others and that will direct the glory to the wonderful grace of God. And that is where the glory belongs."

He casually got up, said perhaps we'll meet again, and left. I found out later that he went to the airport that afternoon and I never saw him again.

I did what he suggested immediately. Studying Biblical leaders and researching other men of God I found them riddled with problems and faults, so much so that people could not worship them, but had to look past them to see God's work in and through them so that He would get the glory. A whole new sense of purpose was injected into my life. It was about to be about doing things for His glory, to deflect accolades from me to Him! My sufficiency was not in me, but in Christ.

But I still struggled with the language. Sitting on the porch drinking vodka or something just as strong, I tried to read a local newspaper. I used my tablet translator, but it took me an hour to read through a two-paragraph article. I ripped the paper to shreds, threw the tablet across the porch, and cussed out God.

"Why the hell did you send me here when I can't learn this damn language?"

And I continued to cry and scream.

Once I had calmed down some, I went to the back bedroom to check email on the computer. A pop-up appeared on the screen titled "How to Speak Spanish—Fast". I clicked it. The website declared "No more grammar, learn to speak". The first sentence it taught was "Yo tengo coche". ("I have a car.")

God answered my outburst. I fell to my knees and asked His forgiveness.

CHAPTER 9
MIRACLE OF THE RESURRECTED TRUCK

At four in the morning a group of us piled into a rusty old van to drive to an area above Ayutla, 5 hours of winding mountain roads in the high Sierra. We met Pastor Gustavo at the base of our last climb. He had rented a large flatbed truck with wooden rails and dual tires as we were going up during the rainy season. There had been no rain for the past four days, so this was a good time to go.

The road came to a 100-foot section of river, which was not very high at this point. The road crossing the river was merely chunks of concrete and rock laid out to make a narrow platform that could only be navigated single file. We decided to leave the van. Everyone climbed into the truck and we proceeded up the last difficult stretch to our destination.

We performed an afternoon and an evening program. The team also visited many individual homes. We finished our last program around 8:30 pm and would have left for Acapulco, but

Miracle of the Resurrected Truck

some people from the village had prepared food and invited us to stay and eat. It would have been rude to refuse. We didn't leave until after 11:00 pm, knowing we wouldn't get back until after 5 or 6 in the morning.

We descended the mountain and came to the river now swollen over its banks. Lightning flashed in the upper mountains during our programs, but we had paid it no mind. Now, water raced over the makeshift bridge.

Gustavo just smiled. As I did not speak much Spanish and he did not speak much English, he nodded his head and drove into the rushing waters. The tires of the flatbed felt for the blocks of concrete. Water rose to the bumper. My heart rose to my throat.

We continued fighting the current another 30 feet or so, when the truck lurched off the solid blocks. But we kept going. Then about midway, the flatbed sank to the door handles. Water flowed through the floor. A flash. A bang. And the engine died.

Gustavo shouted to the group in the back, "¡Canta, suplicar!" (Sing, pray!) He prayed. I began to pray, but I had seen the flash, I knew the engine was engulfed in water, it was already almost over the hood. It was dead. I considered our options—attempt to swim the forceful current or just hang on until morning hoping for the waters to abate.

The prayers continued. The singing intensified with clapping of hands. All more a sound of joy than cries for help. Gustavo, who has a beautiful voice, started singing "How Great Thou Art" in Spanish. I joined in in English. At the end of the psalm, he looked at me and smiled. He looked at the key and turned it. It started immediately. The exhaust from the muffler sounded like a motorboat and the engine made funny noises. Gustavo put it into gear and drove out.

Miracle of the Resurrected Truck

When we got to the shore I opened the door and stepped out with wet feet but full of faith. Praise flowed from our lips, yet I got the impression that they weren't surprised. As for me, I was dumbfounded, my heart was pounding, and the words "how great thou art" flooded my thoughts and feelings.

CHAPTER 10
MEETING SAMMY & PAMELA

Though my frenetic pace had slowed and while I struggled to find purpose, God's work continued, and He knew exactly why I was there.

Hoping to make me feel needed, Pastor Lacko asked me to speak at some established churches close to Acapulco. Most Christian churches in Acapulco have no signs and are extremely small, consisting of one or two small rooms with 15-20 people attending. Generally being open to the street, dogs, chickens, and pigs wander in looking for scraps of food dropped during the time of gathering. Once a pig plopped down near me while I was teaching and had to be carried off, as it would not respond to the nudging of my foot.

It was during this time that I was first put in contact with Ron Lavender, the real estate agent. Ron owned one of the largest, if not the largest, real estate companies in the Acapulco area. He was in his mid-80s and in good health. I visited him and we talked quite a long time. He took me to his sailboat, and I noticed that wherever he went, he was accompanied by an armed guard. Finding this strange for a real estate agent, I asked him about it.

A few years back, he told me, kidnappers took him from his boat and held him captive for a year in a shipping container. They extorted several thousands of dollars from his relatives during this time. Yet God sustained him, and he was eventually released.

Ron put me in touch with Vicky Vasquez. He told me she spoke perfect English and was a professional translator. A little older than I, she was by far the best translator I had come across and her heart shone the light of Jesus wherever she went. Through her I met many friends that were to help us later in this journey.

One of the last places I ministered with Jenny and Saul before they went their separate ways came to be one of the most significant. We were asked to visit a little Assemblies of God mission church on the very top of one of the high hills in the area. And

Meeting Sammy & Pamela

it was a steep hill. Driving up a rough cement road, the tires spun as if on ice or gravel. You could only go so far before you had to get out and walk the remaining 40 feet or so up a little rock-strewn path. And thank God for the rocks to have a foothold. We arrived at a 30' x 40' cement pad with two small cement block buildings at the back. One stored equipment and was kept locked, the other was used for children's classes.

A young couple in their mid-20s lead the small group of 10 or 11 plus the 15 or 16 children. Sammy and Pamela Morales had two small children of their own, the youngest, a year and a half

Meeting Sammy & Pamela

still nursing. I found this a bit of a shock the first few times I preached, seeing 5-10 ladies nursing babies and small children during the service. But this is common in Mexico as formula is unaffordable.

Sammy and Pamela rode buses and walked an hour and a half with their children to do services on Sundays and Wednesday evenings. They visited the little congregation on Tuesdays and on Wednesdays before the service. Their pay consisted of whatever little was collected in the offering plate, usually about 150 pesos— $13 American money.

We fell in love with their spirit and energy and love of Jesus. We planned to visit again the following week and train them to use puppets for children's programs. Jenny and I soon learned that Pamela's skills far exceeded ours. The next week after training she already had a team of young people performing a program with hand-made puppets. Cathedral of Praise, a large church in Charleston, previously donated several large, professionally made puppets to us, so we gave them to the group, and they did a great job setting up a program.

Armed with handmade flyers, we crisscrossed the steep roads inviting people to come see a puppet show. A rope stretched across the back of the slab with sheets hung over it became the stage the youths stood behind to perform. We prayed for God's blessing. We prayed for people to come. We prayed for their salvation. The excitement and the fervency and the genuine concern of these young Christians for the souls of their community greatly inspired us.

The small area could hold about 50 plastic chairs. To our joy, more than 100 arrived to see the puppets. We removed chairs. People simply sat on the cement floor. Others hung over the side of the fence surrounding the slab. I prayed for their safety—a 40-foot drop fell down the edge on the other side.

Sammy instinctively walked through the crowd and one by one introduced himself to everyone, asking their name and if he could come visit with them some time.

Another program soon followed. Small groups were formed, and this little mission grew. And it grew until it could grow no more for lack of space.

CHAPTER 11
MIRACLE OF THE FLAT TIRE

We visited the same village beyond Ayutla. Again, we left to return to Acapulco late at night (you'd think we'd learn), eight of us in the old van loaded with equipment for the program.

I'd heard stories that strangers should not pass through Ayutla on the weekends. The men often traded their wives and daughters for money to drink and party wildly. So, intrepidly we drove around the town to avoid the debauchery.

That's when we noticed the flat. The rear passenger tire was losing air fast. We pulled into a gas station on the edge of town, filled the tank, and changed the tire. The spare gave us trouble. It evidently had been under the van for a very long time, because it was difficult to remove, and it too was flat. The lady running the station did not want us to use the air compressor, she just wanted to go home. A few pesos in her pocket bought us time to fill the tire. But once filled, we could hear the slow hiss of air. Feeling

Miracle of the Flat Tire

around the tire confirmed the leaking air. We filled it again to no avail, the hissing continued. We had to go. Driving away slowly, we hoped to find some place open to fix the tire. It was now after midnight.

Continuing to roll along cautiously, all lights were out, nothing was open. We gradually increased our speed and eventually arrived at a small village. It too was all closed up. It was now 1:00 in the morning and we could still hear the air escaping. We had no choice but to go as far as we could.

We actually made it to Acapulco. Dead tired, we got to the apartment sometime after 6:00. Taking the equipment out of the van, I could still hear the hissing. Impossible.

A tire shop around the corner opened at 8:00, so we took the van and waited. When the man arrived to open, we were there. He checked the tire and heard the air slowly whistling out. We told him the story and his only response, "¡Imposible!" Immediately, the tire went flat.

He removed the tire and effortlessly poked several holes in the sidewall with a screwdriver. That tire was completely dry rotted, yet God kept it inflated on a dangerous night trip until we could get it to this shop. The repairman gave his life to Christ that morning.

CHAPTER 12
EMAILS FROM GOD

Looking back at this time, I recall my stubbornness and aggravation at things not going according to how I thought things should happen. While I backed away from God's plan and asked Him to bless mine, He set people in my path for the future of Mission Acapulco and His work and glory. God had been sending me "emails" about what I should be doing, and who I should be doing it with and for, all along. I either did not see them or ignored them altogether.

What do I mean by an "email" from God? I read my Bible daily and have learned to listen to the Spirit rather than to interpret the text; this I'll do when studying for a sermon or teaching, or for personal intellectual edification. I find these messages from God's Word, often pointed and specific, speak to my personal relationship with God. What I consider to be "emails" are things outside of the Bible from the Lord guiding my direction.

I'm an old man and I have hearing problems, especially when it comes to direct personal correction or doing something that doesn't fit my plans. So, a lot of my emails from God went unnoticed or completely ignored.

Jenny went back to Tulsa, OK and Saul returned to mountain life in Tecpan. I should have seen the signs of their separation, but I was too close. I received less opportunities in the churches. For a while I just taught one or two midday classes and one on Saturdays at a couple of Bible schools. Occasionally, I would preach three or four Sunday services at different churches. All of these were done with the assistance of translators, Vicky being the most prominent, but God had also sent a young woman named Iveth Reyes and a young man named Orlando to help. But after about three months, the invitations dried up. This was an email I ignored.

I again questioned God why He sent me here. I couldn't go out at night for fear of kidnapping and the escalation of the gang wars. Even on the main streets of the tourist district several shootings had ravaged the area in a short span of time.

Now that I wasn't speaking so much, I began to attend Maranatha Presbyterian Church at least once or twice a month. Vicky attended this church and translated for the tourists. Their English service, once well attended, dwindled to about 15 people as the violence in the city increased. During this time at Maranatha, I met several key individuals.

Still wanting something else to do, I spent a week in Ometepec, four hours east of Acapulco, working with Dr. Jerre Freeman and other American doctors of the World Cataract Foundation. These doctors work together to eliminate cataract blindness in the state of Guerrero, Mexico and around the world. There I met the head of Maranatha's Presbytery, an American named Timothy

Wood, whose parents built the first Christian church in that part of Mexico, as well as the Christian hospital we were working in.

I told him we were interested in helping smaller churches grow. He asked me to check on a group of young people working in a small mission in Colosio. Colosio is a small section of the southern end of Acapulco crammed with small (400 sq. ft.) apartments stacked like boxes, as well as individual homes all connected. Of course, crime was rampant. The Presbyterian Church purchased a little daycare center to begin the church of 4 or 5 adults and some children.

In Colosio I met a young doctor and his wife, David and Sarah Monterey. They moved from Mexico City to work in the public hospital system. After sharing stories of our journeys thus far, we felt that we had been called to help this small church grow.

Dr. Monterey and the two elders of the church at Colosio told me I could preach there on a regular basis as long as I had an interpreter. This worked well into "my plan." I worked hard to force myself into this position, because this would take away the unknowns of what I would do next. I had grandiose visions of pastoring this church. I decided to hold a more modern evening service, teaching new praise and worship songs, and some would even raise their hands, something not appropriate in the Mexican Presbyterian culture though I tried to force it. But I was missing something: the ability to lead the people into the neighborhood, to teach them how to share Jesus in the streets. All because I didn't have a grasp on the language.

The Lord eventually sent a young pastor and his wife, and the team of Mission Acapulco performed many programs. The church began to grow. At this point, it had grown to over 70. And they continue to grow by going into the homes, building relationships, and meeting people's needs.

The language barrier was never more apparent to me than when one of the young ladies of the church was kidnapped while visiting her boyfriend in a different city. They kidnapped her not for ransom, but for prostitution. Being a devout Christian, she would not go along with this, so they cut her into pieces and threw them into the street. I knew the family and frustratingly tried to minister to them through a translator. How could I even think to try to minister to them effectively, compassionately, through a translator?

At about the same time, a couple with two teenage boys moved into one of Ms. Vicky's condominiums four floors above me. Mauricio and Linda Corona were teachers and businesspeople who had been persecuted for their faith and came to Acapulco to start a new life. Both bilingual, they worked at a Montessori school—he as a swim coach, she taught English. They gave me books and tried to teach me some basic Spanish. They also provided me with friendship. Being bilingual, they were sympathetic to my thoughts and feelings. And they enjoyed sports, as I do. This email I understood. So, I scaled back my ministry activities to concentrate on becoming better able to communicate in Spanish. This enabled me to talk with the many who came and to assist in following up with contacts.

Many of God's emails spoke of the tremendous gifts of Sammy and Pamela. Using the puppets I had brought from the States, they improved upon the program week to week. They formed a group of teenagers to work the puppets, dance, perform dramas, and help with props. Their program could mesmerize over 200 children in the hot sun for an hour. God's emails should have been clear—get behind these people, support them. But I got distracted.

The budget was tight. Sammy and Pamela received about $20 a week in their church. A trusted friend suggested two people that could help with the work and were in need. So, I split our meager budget three ways. Only one of them had a car; therefore, my duties as taxi driver increased. I slowly began to understand that I was trying to please too many people and not follow the Lord's direction—support the Morales.

This time of transition, about 6 months, bore heavy on me. Again, I felt alone and useless. Again, I asked God what was I doing here. Part of the problem was that I still saw myself doing great and wonderful things in Mexico. I was the one called here, I had the vision, I had left everything. There had to be more to this than what I was seeing. Indeed, God was doing great things; God was setting up a ministry to affect thousands. But I didn't see my current role as being very important and that bothered me. Even though I knew now that I was sufficient in Christ, I wanted something else to do, I really wanted to do more teaching.

Another diversion came in the form of a wonderful homeopathic doctor. Dr. Guillermo had been a rebel leader spending time in prison when God took hold of his heart. Baptized with the fire of the Holy Spirit, he was sent out to plant churches. A work had begun in the mountains of Costa Chica with five missions. Dr. Guillermo built a team and every Saturday held services in each of these five villages. These villages have seen very little change in the last 100 years. On Tuesday evenings, he would train 10-15 people what he wanted them to teach in the villages on Saturday.

I began to go with them and was invited to teach. I planned a 4-part doctrinal series. I could not find an interpreter for that timeframe, so Dr. Guillermo, who spoke some English, interpreted. After three sessions, I was not invited back to complete the fourth. This was confusing and frustrating, after all, I was beginning to have dreams of also teaching in the 5 villages. I later learned that Dr. Guillermo did not understand me and thought I was teaching something in opposition to what he was teaching. We are still good friends and I help them when I can; but again, my role became that of supporter—financially, and in prayer and encouragement to these young evangelists.

CHAPTER 13
UNSELFING

I want to take some time and tell you more specifically what the Lord taught me through my insecurities, doubts, and flaws. The lessons I learned dealt with my "unselfing" and losing "my religion".

I had been reading John's Gospel where John the Baptist told the people that "He must increase, and I must decrease." So, I thought that if I could get enough of me out of the way so that Jesus could show through, to be certain that my decisions and what I taught were totally of Christ, then I would experience pure joy.

I searched the scriptures for help and came upon 2 Corinthians 4:16-18. I saw Paul dealing with personal issues and I could relate. I often felt that when things didn't go my way that I was insufficient for the task, though I knew from Romans 8:28 that even if I screwed up, our gracious God makes no mistakes, and it would be ok. Yet, I still felt a lot of joy, of wholeness, of being ok. That's when I first had a real sense of what the problem may be.

Intellectually I knew about faith, I understood the concept, but what God was telling me was that I was not releasing, or walking, in faith. It wasn't about what I did or thought, but was I trusting Jay's way or the promises of God. In this chapter, Paul is telling the people don't look at us, turn to Christ to see the light.

My process of unselfing began when I accepted my role as God's errand boy. The message, not the errand boy, matters. The work of the errand boy, or as we like to call ourselves leaders, is holding yourself accountable to God to find potential in people and processes. Authority when used to draw attention to self has no place in this role.

I also had to learn not to be afraid of failure. I feared failure and having doubts and did not want to be vulnerable enough to admit this to anyone. I wanted to maintain an image. This killed innovation and progress. I defended my ideas to protect myself from feeling insufficient; and, therefore, did not engage with the team effectively. I began to realize that the "my way or the highway" mentality had to go. Leading by finding potential leaders who could do the work in Mexico proved more effective.

Another area of unselfing involved accepting the fact that we are vessels of clay that get broken and leak. We are human. Viewing myself as the leader of Mission Acapulco made it difficult to be vulnerable and engage with others on an equal basis as fellow human beings. We are all imperfect and the faith I needed to believe God lives and works in and through me should be applied to my fellow believers. Replace the "leader, dictator, very special errand boy" mentality with a willingness for honest engagement, to listen, to compromise for the development of others. Much of my life and ministry I wanted certainty. To enforce my authority, I would tell people that I had prayed hard over actions until I was absolutely certain they were correct. My protection against being wrong. This totally circumvented engagement with others and denied that their thoughts were important.

We must accept the fact that apart from Christ we can do nothing for the Kingdom of God. To know God's will means not knowing <u>about</u> Him, but to <u>know</u> Him. I have extensive spiritual and religious education and know a lot about God, about Christ, about the Holy Spirit, but have I experienced Him as a person in my life? Experiencing who He is allows me to trust Him with total control of my insufficient life. The light at the end of the tunnel appeared.

My attitude changed. People noticed. They began to open up and share their thoughts. Using my organizational skills, we took their ideas and I helped to implement them. We began to work more as a team, and this shift would have far-reaching implications for a more New Testament style church being formed. The Western style of church has been adopted for use in most mission situations and is the reason, I believe, they grow so slowly. My pride hurt a bit, though, and I thought to make my mark yet a different way. I theorized that if I did ministry more the way Jesus had done, we would see greater results. I read the entire book of Luke one night looking for clues. I decided I would take the gospel into the street, not to preach, but to interact and show a loving spirit.

Normally, I would attend three church services every weekend. I took a Sunday off to wander the market and commercial areas surrounding Acapulco. I drove to Colosio with a supply of New Testaments and gospel pamphlets. Here, the makeshift shops come out to the streets. Tables and plastic chairs crowd onto the edge of the road with hundreds of people passing in and out between them.

I knew this area and remembered an elderly man that always sat on the same cement block on the same spot of dirt and concrete road. He didn't appear to be disabled and didn't seem to be begging for money, he simply sat and watched the traffic. I saw him and took this as an opportunity to speak with him.

His genuine smile revealed that he lacked teeth and was in desperate need for mouthwash. It didn't take long to learn (he enjoyed talking) that though his clothes were ragged, he had a place to sleep with his son and daughter. And, I found out, he was a Christian and loved to talk to people about Jesus. I asked if he gave Bibles to the people he spoke with. He explained that most people here did not read, though some could; but even so, he had no Bibles to give. I rushed to my car and brought back about 10 Bibles, for which he was most grateful.

Feeling good, I continued down the street pondering again what would Jesus do here, when I was interrupted by a lady hysterically screaming and crying in front of me. I asked her what was wrong, and she sobbed that she could not find her daughter. She described her as a short little girl in a bright yellow dress, then hurriedly ran off asking others along the way. I continued down the street looking about for her daughter. At the very next alley leading to a group of apartments I saw a little girl in a yellow dress. I hurried to her and told her that her mother was looking for her. She followed me out and when she saw her mother ran quickly to her. Her mother thanked me, and I told her to thank Jesus and gave her a pamphlet.

Hungry, I sat at one of the many tables selling tacos. Though my Spanish was not perfect, but getting better, I would try to share Jesus with anyone else who sat down with me. Most were polite and stayed until I was finished, others immediately walked away. After about three hours in the heat, I was tired. No ebullient, joyous feeling permeated my being, only a sense of satisfaction at having done my duty.

I continued this for three weeks, finding it extremely interesting and filled with many wonderful experiences. But it was hard work and I found not a lot of peace and joy in it. I know that the early church grew because of their excitement over the gospel of the risen Christ. It seems today we spend a lot of resources on collecting people into a building and training them to do "church", instead of being a spontaneously loving group of people sharing our life in Christ.

I spent many hours meditating about my lack of feeling the joyous reward of serving Jesus. I wasn't having fun. It wasn't easy or natural for me. There was no overwhelming sense of urgency or concern for the salvation of others in me. I had worked hard, and I had sacrificed much on this journey to become a missionary. I then noticed that "I" and "me" and "my" occurred frequently in my thoughts. If it wasn't working, perhaps the problem was with me. And so, another time of study and soul-searching and fervent prayer for an answer to unselfing ensued. Something had to be done with me so I would not get in the way and yet still be useful. "Do You care enough about me even at this age to change me?"

CHAPTER 14
STRIPPED OF RELIGION

For a long time, it has been my habit to read my Bible in the morning and evening with a notebook at hand. I read not to interpret, but to hear God speak to me. Sometimes for five to six minutes, at other times a session may last an hour or more. I do not close my eyes, bow my head, nor get on my knees; but as I write notes about what I hear from my heavenly Father, I discuss it with Him. To me, this is quite different from the emails from God. With the emails I must decide how to receive them: do I accept the person, like the person, listen to them, use them in the work, or just enjoy their friendship. The things I hear from God concerning me are absolute. I really don't want to agree with the things I read in God's Word concerning me, but I have to. Yet, in my quest to feel the reality of God in my life, was this just another religious activity to attain it?

Stripped of Religion

I have filled over 60 notebooks, many of which are highly personal messages that I do not feel comfortable sharing. I will pick a few relevant notes and passages.

I find the Message Remix easiest for me to understand. In my readings, I would often switch between a book in the Old Testament, followed by a book in the New. It amazed me how the messages paralleled each other—the prophets speaking to the people of Israel, the words of Jesus and the apostles to the Christians of that day, all speaking to me.

After finishing Jeremiah, I decided to return to the Gospels. When God impresses something on my mind, I usually stop and talk to Him about it, then write it down. I spent quite a bit of time in Matthew chapter 5 and heard "live generously and free" over and over again. I understand this to mean giving of yourself for the benefit of others and I felt that, in some ways, I was doing that. But the context is one of joy, of lightness of heart, of happily being a generous person. And not just money, though that's implicit, also sharing grandly everything you have.

As this precept firmly pressed upon my mind, I tried to increase my generosity. By nature, I am not the most generous person in the world, and I like to hold onto things, even things that others, including the ministry, could really use. For example, when we purchased portable speakers from Fender, a sizable order, they included a very nice guitar. Now Sammy's guitar was quite old, and it would have been nice for him to be able to replace it. This new guitar was so pretty; I feared it would be scratched up in the places we traveled, especially on the mountain roads. I held onto that guitar for a long time. And then when I did give, I felt that I fulfilled my duty, but there was no joy in it.

I stalled in chapter 6 of Matthew for a while. I was being told to examine the work I was doing to see if God was being exalted, or was I trying to look important. Examining my motives, I realized there were things in me I had no idea how to correct. How would people look at me and my team and see God? I heard some people say, "great program" and occasionally someone would say "glory to God". The sad thing is I enjoyed hearing the former the most.

Matthew 7 impressed upon me the need to 'put others first'. I consciously try to do this because I know this to be problem area for me. But the harder I tried the more frustrated I would get. I found no joy in it.

Chapters 10 and 11 spoke to me about 'working the neighborhood, impacting the community', followed by chapter 12 telling me to 'check the fruit'. I noticed that when Jesus worked the neighborhood, He was redemptive. He healed, taught, fed, and comforted. Checking my fruit, I did find that some had been delivered by God's grace through the teaching of the Word from severe depression and other things. An impact on that community? I wasn't sure what that meant.

The message I got form chapter 14 of Matthew, 'put yeast in people'. The Word of God makes things grow, change, multiply. I discussed this with several others. What type of yeast were we putting in people and were we seeing results? We discovered that we were seeking decisions for Christ but failed to continue to teach by word and example how to be like Christ as a redemptive force in their community. We showed no interest in the real problems these people face daily. Jesus ministered to the needs of the people and that would have an effect on the community.

The Lord encouraged me in the book of Mark. He made clear that He would accomplish all in spite of me. He graciously used our ideas and plans to help many people.

Continuing into the book of Luke, I was shown to 'keep the message simple'. That was important for me, as I love to study and debate theology. Jesus' teachings were clear and simple. We complicate it.

More instruction in Luke included 'ministering to the total person'. Perhaps we needed to be involved with health and welfare ministries as well. With unemployment over 50%, we were moved, with the help of our friends in the Jewish community, to get a truckload of used clothes for single parents to sell in the area. This continues to this day as a source of income to these families, and a source of redemption for the community.

It seems to me the goal of most missions here in Mexico, and quite possibly other countries, is to find enough people to gather for church services. Without a building to meet in on a regular basis you can't be successful. To acquire a building, you need money. And when the focus becomes money for a building so people can hear a sermon the focus goes to middle- and upper-class people, and the poor are left on the sidelines or become projects to soothe our conscious. I know of one denominational leader who tells his pastors that if they don't focus on people with money, they will never have a church. I recall that I used to get excited when anyone who could write a sizable check showed interest in our little church in Michigan.

Do not get me wrong. I am not taking away the importance of church. In Hebrews we are admonished to come together to encourage one another, to make our lights shine brighter to make a difference, a redemptive difference in the community. This can be accomplished in homes. No, I'm not so sure that a church building is God's ultimate goal for a community. I am convinced that there is more to spreading the gospel than to raise a building for us to preach at people. In the gospels we see Jesus hanging out with the poor, with regular folks. He paid attention to them. So, we examined our work. Who were we talking to? Who did we visit? Who were we making friends with?

Now God spoke more to me about being a friend. Oftentimes, when introducing myself or being introduced, it was as the missionary from the United States. In a formal setting this may be fine, but on the front porch of a little shack it sounds pretentious. This separates me from them—I am a person of importance; therefore, you should listen to me.

Looking at the life of Jesus, the Son of God, He spoke with authority, but reading between the lines, I believe He was a good companion. I think people loved to be in His presence. Unfortunately, the same cannot always be said of me. Instead of loving people as Jesus loved, I tend to infer that I have a message and whether you like me or not is unimportant. You must listen and respond. This is far from being redemptive in a community.

I related to the team God was building in the same way. They needed knowledge and leadership, but rather than building them up in a nurturing relationship, I preferred having control and being an authoritarian. This attitude pushed away some very capable people, for which I am sorry for to this day.

At another time, God spoke very clearly to me from Luke 8:10, a passage I have oftentimes read to unbelievers. His message to me was different. He showed me that I did not understand the pleading voices of the people in these villages, in these incredibly poor communities. My eyes and ears were closed. My interests lie in one thing: get these people to believe in Jesus and their problems would be solved. I struggled (and continue to

Stripped of Religion

struggle) with identifying the real needs within a community; how to be used by Jesus to affect a total area with His redeeming presence.

It occurred to me that the secret was to be like Jesus. I tried. I was bad at it. It wasn't natural. It was hard.

Then I read the wonderful story of Jesus standing on the Mount of Olives looking over Jerusalem and weeping. He wanted so much for these people. His chosen people who sacrificed a lamb every year waiting for His coming; yet now that He was here, they rejected Him.

The area I work within the city of Acapulco has a beautiful tourist area along the ocean. Half a mile beyond that utter poverty, crime, and police corruption dominate the mountains and valleys. Upon the sides of the mountains you see the thousands of habitations built one atop another. Looking out are great views of the city and the bay of Acapulco. My previous response, "What a gorgeous sight, let's take some pictures." After reading this, I began to feel sorry and inadequate; insufficient to help this mass of humanity living in terrible conditions.

I'm confused about how much social work we should be involved in. I thought of ways to raise money for more food, but you could never raise enough money to feed all these people. What was Jesus teaching? What was His example? He fed and healed many who came to hear His words, by His very nature of love, demonstrating to them a world ruled by love. His mission was inviting people to be a part of the Kingdom of God. He taught and exemplified that as a part of the Kingdom, our Heavenly Father would care for us even as He cares for the birds of the air or the lilies of the field. He also promised them that His love would keep them through the troubles of this world, and they would not be overcome.

So, we concentrated on inviting people into a relationship with Jesus without promising solutions to their problems of poverty. We shared the message of becoming citizens of His Kingdom and not being a part of this world. When people committed their lives to Christ, though their circumstances did not immediately change, their hearts brought them together and they shared with one another. I suspect this is how God takes care of us. He fills us with His love and that love freely gives to others of the household of faith that are in need.

Another time looking down on the city from the mountain, I had a different depressing thought. Walking through the streets I see a lot of sad people; I also see a lot of happy and friendly people. And I think, "If I hear them say the words that they accept Christ, then they would be like me." But I was having so many personal struggles that some of them would be happier without Christ than I was with Christ. Again, feeling insufficient, not being enough. Shame swept over me. Shame is dangerous to live with; it makes you disconnect from people. Apart from my interaction with the team God was building, I was becoming a loner. The Lord sent many wonderful people into my life as friends, yet more and more I kept these contacts to a minimum, and then only as related to the mission. Many nights I pleaded with God to make me whole, to give me what I needed mentally and physically to feel that I was enough. I begged Him to take away the sense of insufficiency and give me a sense of pride in being His child.

Continuing to study the book of Luke, I found a lot of instruction on religion. Again, this paralleled Jeremiah. Clearly, unless I help the poor, feed the poor, love the poor, God will not accept my praise, worship, or other religious deeds. This actually affirmed me, as we were trying to feed the hungry and care for the poor. Though we tried to do the right thing, we didn't always do it constructively and may have caused some dependency. More than a few would come to the services simply for food. And maybe that was okay.

I started having more and more problems with my religion. I always went to church; but now it was becoming clear to me that it was out of sense of duty, not because I wanted to. I felt it pleased God for me to go, and I certainly wanted to please God.

When I was in the States, I enjoyed church. I enjoyed the corporate praise and worship. I enjoyed the fellowship of other believers. I sometimes even enjoyed the sermons. In my opinion, many preachers preach way too long. I think they like to hear their own voice and give out a lot of information to forget. I know I did this when I pastored. Once, I gave a quiz on the sermons of the previous two Sundays: only 10% of what I taught had been retained. That's when I started keeping sermons under half an hour.

But here in Mexico, even though my speaking Spanish was greatly improved, it was still difficult for me to understand, as Spanish speakers speak very fast. I could read and sing the music, but only understand 25-40% of the message. I wondered if I was merely performing a religious exercise every Sunday and continued to disconnect.

The messages I heard in my reading were not getting any better and my attitude clouded my hearing what God was really saying. In Luke 10 and 11 God was clear, 'Let Me lead'. I really wanted that to happen. How do I become totally submissive to the will of God? How do I let Him lead in all things?

I remember finding some comfort in Luke 11. Jesus said He 'would not leave me to the enemy, He would protect me'. Knowing that kept me seeking after more reality in my life. But I still did not understand how God protected me. I still had so much sin in my thought life; and it did not get better, it only got worse. "Are You in me? How can I get authority over these sinful thoughts?" In Luke 11:26, He gave me specific warning about 'trying to fix myself', which is what I was trying to do.

And then once again at the end of chapter 11 the words 'give generously; give happily, crazily'. I look back at the thousands of classes and sermons I have preached, yet I have not been generous with my life to those in need. The fruit that God desires was lacking. God gave me a gift for speaking and I can manipulate an audience well, but that does not matter in God's economy. My religion was useless. God encourages and praises action from a pure heart doing the work of Jesus. I began to realize what both the Old and New Testament say about religion that does not redemptively change the world—it's just religion, it's not a relationship.

Now quite stripped of religion, other than morning and evening prayers, I felt quite lost. Where do I go from here to find the reality of a genuine, happy, heartfelt drive to help others as Jesus in this world?

Even though I continued to endure personal struggles attaining intimacy with Jesus Christ, I worked harder than I believe I ever had in my life. A lot of work I could have said no to, but I was driven; I was convinced that if I worked hard enough and saw the results of God's hand in people's lives, I would find myself closer to feeling Jesus controlling my life.

My days were packed preparing messages, teaching classes, preaching, traveling in the mountains, building a sustainable team. Up at 5:30, breakfast of fruit and toast, Bible reading and devotions. Study until 1:00 or 2:00 in the afternoon. Almost every day, 2 or 3 events. Returning home, study until midnight, as well as devotions. I worked myself into exhaustion trying to feel enough, to sense wholeness, to see Jesus in my life.

Stripped of Religion

I preached 3 or 4 messages every weekend with Sammy and Pamela (who continued to do their "muppet" shows better and better), I really didn't understand how difficult these pastors had it. Trying to feed their families by driving a taxi or working in a store or whatever just to put food on the table. These pastors work harder than anyone I know. They are not put on pedestals; they are looked down upon by their society. Yet, after working 10 hours a day, 6 days a week, they would try to visit all the new contacts we developed.

Very few churches in the area can support the pastor. This makes it a struggle for a lot of them to just invite people to their church instead of forming relationships. But I see them starting these churches and missions out of the love of Christ flowing out of them. Though they looked to me for teaching, they taught me. I saw the spontaneous love that I felt I forced or did from a sense of duty.

I also learned from the doctors who volunteered for the World Cataract Foundation. The best cataract surgeons in the world dedicated to work under difficult circumstances with subpar equipment. Still, they would perform over several hundred surgeries in a week. Some brought their own nurses with them. This meant that their own clinics and offices were closed, yet they continued to pay the salaries of those that came with them. They worked long, hard hours and at the end of the day slept in tiny rooms with no air conditioning. No one complained. They were happy giving and giving in the name of Jesus of their gifts and talents. Each of these doctors came from varying denominational backgrounds with different doctrines from mine, but they were filled with joy and satisfaction. I felt that I was doing the same and had given a lot, but I was not experiencing the same joy.

It began to dawn on me that I had been trying to be the leader, the one others could look to and find inspiration. Yet as I continued to study the Scriptures I found, especially in the life of the disciples, that they had to learn to follow before they found spontaneity, joy, and power in leading. It was given to me to see that until they truly proclaimed Jesus as "my Lord and my God" that they became ready and willing to wait for instruction before moving.

Once again I was driven to my knees and back to the cross to see how much Jesus loved me. This turning point opened my eyes to see that our only mediator really is Jesus Christ and our only power to accomplish anything is through the Spirit. My pride and my flesh wanted me to be a great leader, yet the true perspective was that I was only one piece of the puzzle in this mission work to which I was sent. I needed to be thankful for the opportunity to be a piece.

So, by surrendering to the leadership of God, it took from a position of leadership to being a part of the body of Christ functioning together to accomplish His will and His work.

You can't image the release of pressure I felt. I now began to find joy in service. I looked at other pieces of this puzzle as total equals that I could not function without. Co-workers and friends noticed a change. I listened more and talked less. I found joy in playing a supporting role and in the successes of others. When one wins, we all win. My admiration, and empathy, for the hardworking, loving pastors who give everything to spread the gospel in their villages grew tremendously. God had gotten me to my place and the work moved further forward as He brought new leadership and solidified others into the workforce.

CHAPTER 15
SAMMY & PAMELA

I now worked hard to train the pastors to build relationships with their neighbors and those that came to the programs. It's too easy for them to just invite people to come to their church, hoping for a few more pesos in the collection plate. Certainly, they deserved to be paid, but they tended to be pushy about church with no mention of a relationship with Jesus.

Sammy and I would take a day or two during the week and visit people with the pastor. They would follow directions the first time, but the next time would just ask them to come to a program. Relationships were not being built.

So, I spent a good bit of time with Sammy and Pamela teaching them the basics of home visitation. They are both extremely outgoing and Sammy has a wonderful gift of communication. When we visited a home, I learned to sit back and listen. I finally realized that my efforts needed to be focused on training and sharing as much knowledge as I could to allow these people to carry on the work in Mexico in their way. This prepared us for the next steps.

One of the big problems facing us at the time was that I had the only vehicle, a 2001 Ford Escape. It took quite a beating driving it into the mountains as much as we did. Six or eight people, speakers, and other equipment crammed together for trips up to two hours or more on those wonderful mountain roads.

The little church Sammy pastored was about 6 or 7 miles from where they lived with his father in the mountains of Saint Augustine on the backside of Acapulco. Driving to his home was difficult even for me and during the rainy season impossible.

I believe I've mentioned the arduous journey Sammy and Pamela must take with their two children in tow just to get to their church. A pickup truck taxi with a covered back carried them to catch a bus. The buses are old school buses with missing fenders, broken windows, holes in the floors, and black exhaust fumes belching out the back. At a total cost of 13 pesos (about $1.30 per person, including the children), this was more than they could afford each trip. Getting off the bus, each carrying a child, they would walk the last mile and a half up the steep hill to the church.

One day while waiting to meet them at the church, I looked down that steep stretch and saw them struggling up, soaked in sweat, smiles on their faces, anticipating a couple hours of practice for the next program. About halfway up, God spoke very clearly to my heart that no matter what we were to get them a car. I had no idea how this would be possible, but I didn't question and determined to tell them.

When they reached the last mud stone step, I put my hands on each of their shoulders, looked them in the eyes, and said "God is going to make it possible for you to have a car in the next two weeks."

My statement surprised even me.

I had $800 in my savings account about 9000 pesos. I could not find a functioning car for that amount. I shared my dilemma with Ms. Vicky, and she said she could match my $800. That's when God sent me an "email", a young man who spent a lot of time in Canada and so helped translate when he could. His father was selling a car, a 1970 VW bug, for 20,000 pesos. There are hundreds of these on the roads in the area, mainly used for taxis. We negotiated a final price of 16,000 pesos.

We picked up Sammy and Pamela without telling them what we were doing and took them to sign the paperwork. This was the first car they had ever owned and to say that they felt a tremendous sense of blessing would be an understatement. I remember with fondness one time counting nine people, two speakers, and two speaker stands packed into that car.

So, in spite of my personal struggles to get closer and more intimate with Christ, God moved and worked in many marvelous ways to further the ministry and impact of Mission Acapulco.

Now that Sammy and Pamela had a car, things were easier for me. It also gave them more energy. Sammy continued to pastor the little church he founded, and it grew nicely. One day, he told me he was training another pastor and asked if I would help with the process. He wanted to leave the church in his hands so he could work fully with Mission Acapulco. He loved that he could reach more people with the Gospel. His constant concern has been how best to use his talents for the Kingdom of God, and he has many. Teaching, preaching, playing and providing instruction for several instruments, and counseling; most all natural talent and self-taught skills.

About this time, I had given Sammy one of my computers, and with two others he found, he started an internet café. You can see these on just about every street corner. Few people own computers, less have printers. Some appeal to a wealthy person to buy the computers for them, but then most of the profits are paid to that person. And then there's the black tax—extortionists.

One evening, a pounding at their door shook the house and their hearts. "You will pay us 5000 pesos or tomorrow you and your family die!"

These are not idle threats. I know a little bakery that sold tortillas whose owners had been killed in front of their two children for not paying on time. Friends, who sold clothing from a tent stall, had to shut down because of threats. They witnessed others gunned down in front of their business.

I was angry. If I had had my shotgun, I would have waited for them to return. Instead, I went to the local federal police station. I found someone in charge who spoke English, explaining that these men who had threatened Sammy were the same men who killed the owners of the tortilla shop. I told him I would be willing to go with them.

"Well," he said, "we are very busy here and really don't have time to help. The best thing for them to do is move."

We packed everything they owned—a plastic table and chairs, a couple mattresses, a box of children's toys, their clothes, and a medium-sized box of dishes, silverware, and 2 or 3 pots and pans—and moved them into a 12' x 12' cement block room in the back of the church.

I couldn't sleep. We needed to do something for them. I contacted Dr. Monterey and others and told them what had happened. Together, we found an apartment for them that cost $250/month. At the time, we were paying Sammy about $300/month. We recently had stopped paying a couple of part-time workers, so with that money we now paid their rent. The apartment actually came with some furniture and an air conditioner in the upstairs bedroom, all extra blessings.

About six months later, the two extortionists were involved in a shootout and both killed. Now able to return to his father's house, they made plans to build a cement block house of their own.

Sammy sent his resignation to the church to start working full-time with Mission Acapulco. We then started paying Sammy $1000/month, though he still needed to supplement his income by teaching music classes and doing an evening service at a Presbyterian church every week.

Now that Sammy and Pamela were full-time, we made big changes to the program that expanded the ministry tremendously. They had developed a team of talented young people that assisted with most of our programs. Pamela trained them, quite professionally, I think, to do dramas that she wrote. These dramas kept people spellbound. With the addition of their car, we were able to do more, especially in the back of the city.

When traveling into the mountains, we used part of the team, so we only needed one vehicle. This young team was thrilled to travel the 3 or 4 hours to these indigenous villages. Lacking money and transportation, most of them had never left the city. The same was true for Sammy and Pamela, this was all very new and exciting. Both were raised in poverty, living in housing that makes our project homes look like exclusive gated communities. Neither of their families had ever travelled either.

But their love for people is incredible. I remember one time giving Sammy 100 pesos because I knew they needed food. He had been asked to visit an old crippled lady in the back mountain on his way home. We had a hard time finding her, but when we did, and we visited with her and her husband for a time, our hearts broke. These people looked starved to death. Sammy quietly slipped the husband the 100 pesos, told him to buy some food, and he would visit them the next week.

100 pesos, less than $10, could buy them 1 kg, about 2 pounds, of tortillas and a bag or two of beans. A lot of them have some chickens, sometimes living in the house, so they are able to get a few eggs every day and that's what they live on. I recall the

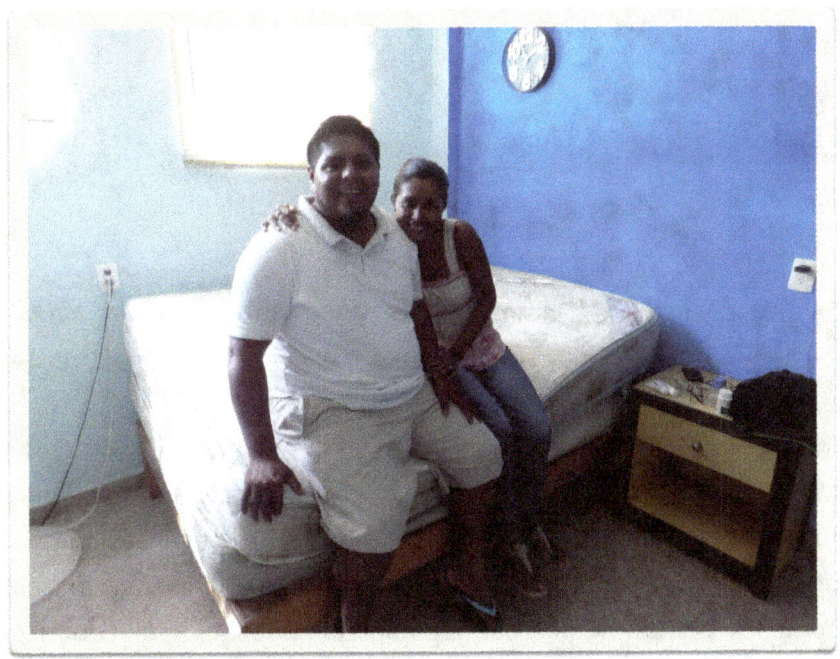

first time I took Sammy and Pamela to a nice restaurant. They were giddy with excitement. They dressed in the best they had, and their beaming faces said it all. When Sammy teaches on faith, he sometimes alludes to these experiences—owning a car, having a place to live, going to a nice restaurant—and points out that if you lift your hands and praise to God, thank Him for what you do have, all things are possible.

CHAPTER 16
QUIET TEARS

Now full-time, Sammy was quite eager to share what he felt needed to be done to make the work more effective. By now, the puppet show's professional presentation got them invited to do a show on the local television program "Good Morning, Acapulco." Though they spent the better part of every Friday doing this and did not receive any pay, the advertising generated for the Mission was priceless. They still do this, and a cable company is showing interest. We hope to negotiate a fair contract.

But what they felt was really needed was more time with each church for quality training to make a more meaningful difference. We brainstormed and decided to do three programs in two-week intervals with each church.

The first would be the puppet show. This would be held on the streets or at the public cement slab court that the government erects in almost every little community or village. We have had over 500 people come to these programs at a time.

The second part of the program would be a movie night with popcorn and drinks. We showed two movies, one for adults and one for children using two projectors and speakers facing opposite directions. In small locations, we might only have 150 or so show, but many new contacts came through these programs.

In between the programs, Sammy and I would work with the pastor and leaders of the church, helping them to learn how to develop relationships and show the love of Jesus to these contacts. We consistently saw these churches grow 10-15% after these programs.

The third program consisted of a dinner and, if a doctor was available, a health night. A simple dinner of hot dogs, chips, a drink, and sometimes a dessert would be followed by a program put together by Sammy and Pamela. Using members of the local church, it would be a time of singing, testimonies, and one or two

dramas. Sammy would also get the congregation involved by contributing plates and cups, and often times, the drinks and popcorn. This gets everyone to take part. During the program, the pastor and leaders could move about, sit with people they didn't know, and just be a friend and talk about whatever; not just trying to convince them to come to their church.

We developed a series of questions for the pastors and leaders. We put these to them one month after the programs to track their effectiveness and to make any necessary changes to the programs.

Around this time, we began to work in an area called Palenque, about 5000 people living in tiny apartments along muddy, broken concrete streets in the valley between the mountains of Saint Augustine. Few businesses survive the extortionists. There is only a small Catholic mission. And it is very hot. Sammy and

Pamela live just up the mountainside and have a heart to build in this area, but more than just a church, a community center. A man from Mexico City owned a small house there and allowed us to begin the work there.

We tried to get pastors that did not have a church to start here. Some people taught a Bible study and others took care of children that were coming. We filled the upstairs with clothing sent to us by the Jewish community in Mexico City and some of the ladies would sell it on the streets.

Actually, it was a huge Walmart-sized parking lot where the ladies spread blankets on the hot asphalt. Hundreds of blankets, inches apart, heaped with used clothes. The heavy odor of sweat and soiled diapers hung in the air. Mothers nursing children would sit in the hot sun all day to sell to the many people who could not afford to purchase from regular clothing stores. The constant back and forth bartering over the hand-me-downs competed with the sound of taxis and buses speeding through the nearby intersection. A few had scrounged up tables and chairs to sell from the coveted outer perimeter of the parking lot, closest to foot and vehicle traffic. These were there every day and tended to sell more, making a nice profit for themselves.

Eventually, the extortionists got wind of the operation and came through to collect. Pounding tables and scattering clothes, they demanded their tax. The makeshift merchants stood fast and refused. Shots rang out, silencing the bartering. Six people were fatally shot, and all their money taken. Meanwhile, on the street corner nearby void of traffic lights, police directed cars through the intersection unconcerned. They had been seen earlier conversing with the extortionists.

The selling stopped for about two weeks, but of necessity the women began to return. I remember one young lady, Analuis, on her first day selling clothes. I had been to her home on a previous occasion. She had 4 children and only a bottle of water in the refrigerator.

She took the children with her. Where else could they go? The two babies packed into a child's toy stroller were draped with a blanket to shade them from the hot sun. The five-year-old helped stack and arrange the clothing while she held the toddler. Her bartering skills were amazing. She dealt skillfully all day and brought in 500 pesos.

When the day was done, she came to me and pulled a sweaty change purse from her bosom and handed me the 500 pesos. "Here is the money for the church, Señor Jay."

I said, "No, dear, 75% of this money is for you. God is paying you."

She stared at me uncomprehending. I tried to hand the pesos to her, but she stood motionless. I had to take her hand and place the money in it. She stared at the money in her hand as quiet tears slipped down her cheek.

"What's wrong, child?" I asked.

She looked up at me, her expression unchanged, tears still flowing, and simply said, "Now I buy food for my children."

CHAPTER 17
THE PROCLAIMER

When I first came to Mexico, I would ask everyone I met if they had a Bible. It seemed 9 out of 10 did not. So, I gave away cases of Bibles thinking I was accomplishing great things sowing all this seed. Unfortunately, less than half of these people could read, let alone understand the language of the printed Word. To help with this problem, we found a recorder called "The Proclaimer", a recording of the Bible done dramatically using voice actors, music, crowd noise and other effects. This could be set in a front yard or middle of a public area and let Jesus do the teaching and preaching.

These people are very susceptible to strange sects and religions because they do not know what the Word of God actually says. They must rely on what the pastors and priests tell them it says. This way they get to hear it for themselves. If we do any teaching afterwards, we never go beyond what the Scripture passage that they have just heard teaches.

Now that Sammy and Pamela had more time, they began visiting areas with "The Proclaimer". They would go on Thursdays to a group of little houses built 30 feet from the road and play a chapter from the Gospels while people sat outside on the patch of dirt in front of their homes. Afterward, Sammy would play his guitar and sing a song with everyone. It amazed me how they would listen to that recording with intense concentration. Within a month of using "The Proclaimer" we needed to rent a larger building for services.

Oh, the effectiveness of the Word of God! The Spirit and the teaching of Jesus far surpasses the attempts of men to push their denominational doctrines and agendas. It is a Living Word that does not need to be added to or bloated with explanation, as it was written for common people. We hope to have more of these to further share and expand the Kingdom, watching as the Sword of the Spirit changes lives and builds His church.

We have not found anyone willing to ship "The Proclaimer" into Mexico because they are made in China and the duty charged by the Mexican government is extremely high. We are desperately looking for ways to get more or to find another less expensive means. The people recognize the authority of the Bible and are hungry to hear, frequently asking for more.

CHAPTER 18
FOLLOWING GOD'S DIRECTION

It is important that we stay in a following mode as opposed to a speculative mode when determining the correct direction for the future of Mission Acapulco. It is imperative for the board in the States, and more so the board and leaders in Mexico, to constantly practice listening to God's voice. In the early years of the mission, God led in spite of my problems, inadequacies, and downright stubbornness. As I changed, the work grew into a positive impact on one of the most violent parts of Mexico.

On a budget of $1000 a month, Mission Acapulco has impacted 35 or more areas of the surrounding region. Growth continues as the team walks in faith through doors God opens.

In every new area, the team is responsible for finding and training new leaders. This presents a challenge to supplement the income of these new leaders, allowing them time to minister. It often takes two people spending 60-70 hours a week to gain a small income (anywhere from 7¢/hour to $5/day) for basic needs

Following God's Direction

for their families. Just $200 a week for most would allow them to do God's work full-time. I often feel guilty that we cannot provide God's workers at least a living wage. They're not seeking houses or cars or retirement or even healthcare, only enough to eat.

It is amazing how God continues to bring new leaders who will go through training, sacrificing precious time. They persist because they are excited about sharing with these beleaguered people that they can become citizens of another country, a home in heaven. They do not look for what they can receive on this earth but are intentional in using their talents and resources to lay up treasure in heaven.

Gustavo Franco is one such leader. He is a friend and coworker of Sammy. He is a Bible school graduate and an excellent teacher and preacher. His wife runs a little restaurant serving breakfast. His son is a teacher, and his daughter wants to be a teacher. Gustavo works hard for the Kingdom of God and will do anything for it. He even climbs electric poles to "plug" into the lines to provide electricity for the programs. (That's how they do it down there.)

There are two ways that we determine where God wants us to go next. Word has spread of the work of Mission Acapulco. Pastors or small groups of Christians with a heart for their community come to us asking for help. After prayer, we plan with them to spread the Gospel in their area. They are not coming for a handout, as often as not, our assistance costs them in extra expenses, such as food, printing flyers, and fixing up a place for the programs. These small groups of 10-15 people invest and sacrifice time and resources to set up the programs and to effectively follow-up.

The other way we determine God's direction is to drive or walk through an area looking for churches. If no church is present, we look for individual Christians to talk to. This is very exciting, as God speaks clearly, and Sammy and I seem to know simultane-

ously where to work. Many times, the first person we speak with is a brother or sister in the Lord who has wanted to start a Christian church in their village or area and have a place we can meet. We then do the programs, find and train pastors, leaders, and the right people for various ministries to continue the work. It is such a joy to surround them and support them and help to make contacts, knowing that God will bless the work.

This type of church planting presents us with an issue that we are earnestly seeking the will of God. These churches have no affiliation with other Christians or denominations. Understand, that villages may only be 5 miles apart, but with few people having transportation and the roads often merely trails, it may as well be 100 miles apart. We do not want to leave an opening for Satan to deceive these young churches with false doctrine, nor do we intend to begin another denomination. We are considering a federation of independent churches agreeing that the Bible is the ultimate rule of our faith and life, that can occasionally gather to encourage one another in the Word, to study, learn, and fellowship, to support one another with prayer, and get to know the needs within their area.

CHAPTER 19
PALENQUE

In the area where we work, a building is not necessary except during the rainy season. Generally, for protection from the rain or sun, four poles are put in the ground with a framework of branches, wood, or whatever can be found with a tarp stretched over the top. I find that churches focused on building fancy worship centers drain much of their resources from the true purpose of the church.

Yet our need for a training center began to become clear. I sat in front of Sammy's house as the sun began to rise in the cool of the morning. I asked the Lord about this, as well as a place to provide temporary shelter for the many abused women we come across. And we wanted some place for those in the ministry from far off to be able to spend a night or two for training; nothing fancy, just a place to hang a few hammocks.

Palenque

It was then I thought I heard God say to look at the property right in front of my eyes: a large, open field, graded and flat, with a partially finished two-story block home.

I woke Sammy and asked him about the property. His father lived on the first floor, but he groggily thought he would be happy for Mission Acapulco to use it. After looking into it, we found that we could not outright buy it. The land is within 35 km of the coast and is actually owned by the government, though it can be leased and subleased. We reached a consensus to pay Sammy's father $300/month, money that could fund a bit of retirement. He would continue to live on the first floor, and we would finish off the upstairs with money from churches in the area. We could have full use of the field, and eventually, add a pole building for another church.

But I hadn't actually heard from God on this. We were getting ahead of Him; His plan was much bigger.

While talking with David Monterey about the situation in Palenque, he said he had a cousin who owned a tiny house that we could possibly use. And by tiny, I mean tiny. The bathroom was essentially a closet with a toilet. Narrow steps that a grown man could barely fit through while climbing them on the balls of his feet led to two bedrooms upstairs.

Three young ladies who were a part of the group—Analaura, Analuis, and an older lady that came when she could—wanted to learn English, so we decided to use this place for that purpose. A couple more ladies started coming, so we incorporated a Bible study. Before long, there were fifteen people packed into the tiny living area. I purchased 15-18 plastic chairs and we took the meetings outside to the tiny front yard. Ten to fifteen children packed into each upstairs bedroom for a Sunday school, but the temperatures were so extreme in those unventilated rooms that I insisted they meet on the curb as well.

Students from the Bible school came to help with the services by playing guitar or teaching a short lesson. But when they realized we could only pay them 50 pesos to help with gas money, none returned. No one wanted to build in this area, no one was interested. I asked Sammy if he could do something on Sunday nights, as he was still doing some ministry at his church at this time.

There were so many attending now that we moved the service to the end of the dead-end street near the edge of a cliff. We arranged with the last family on the street to pay for the use of their electricity for a couple of hours. We set up speakers and started later in the evening as the sun went behind the mountain.

We started each service with praise and worship and then a simple Bible study. The church had grown to 40 or more regular adult attendees each week. After the service, those who could contributed money or food. The ladies would cook chili and tortillas, occasionally with rice, and on special occasions pieces of chicken. Large buckets would be filled with a weak colored water.

Several Catholic families lived in the neighborhood. Not wanting to be seen participating in a "Protestant" service, they would sit behind the screen doors of their homes and listen. We tried to visit with them, and though they would not talk with us, they continued to listen each week.

The rainy season approached. Complaints were now being filed that we made too much noise and were hurting the business of some who had stores in front of their homes. We looked at a lot of buildings and finally found a small store on the main street. This offered us a little more room, but the owners would not agree to a long-term commitment.

A dusty road ran a few feet from the all glass front of the store. It was a decent size for us to meet in, about 30' x 30', but when the afternoon sun shone through, this had to be the hottest building I had ever been in in my life. I had to tie a rag around my wrist to keep the sweat from running onto my Bible and notes. Yet, we experienced growth while baking in this place. Many came to know Jesus here. God brought several wonderful people who are still leaders of this church today.

One Sunday when we came to worship at our regular time, someone else occupied the building. This is not unusual for someone to offer a little more money and have a space rented right out from under you.

Having no place to go, we again met in the open until we found a piece of land on top of a hill that had been leveled off.

Palenque

One day, I saw a man working on a bulldozer next to this vacant property. I asked if he knew the owner. He wouldn't give me any contact information but said he would have them contact me from Mexico City. A couple days later, I received a call from Mexico City from a man who sounded very much like the man I spoke with on the bulldozer. He claimed to be the owner and would rent the property to us for 2000 pesos/month, and that we could start using it after he received the first month's rent. I pressed for a meeting with him and other leaders of the church to work out a signed agreement. He said he would just send a receipt. When I told him that we needed to talk to a lawyer, he hung up and we haven't heard from him since.

Sammy also found someone claiming to be the owner. The land was apparently designated for a road, but no one else seemed to know anything about it. He told Sammy to just go ahead and use it. So we did.

We dug holes in the ground for poles and put tin sheeting up for shade. The hill is very steep, so with pickaxes we carved steps in the hard dirt up one side, and embedded tires filled with dirt down the other for easier access. Shipping crates became the platform.

Surrounded by footpaths connecting all the little communities, the church flourished. We provided food at every service, including from a few vendors who would come to make a couple pesos. Ten to fifteen salvations a week was not uncommon. More poles and leaky tin roofs were added. A successful cheesemaker gave us the use of a house 15 feet down the steep bank. The house was riddled with bullet holes fired at point blank range while this man was inside. Miraculously, he escaped unharmed. Though not a believer, he knew that God had protected him and allowing us use of the building was his way of thanking the Lord for sparing his life. We later visited him in his heavily guarded home to present him with his own Bible, which he held fast to his chest as he wept.

Though we did not know the future use of this property on top of the hill, there was now a stable base to work and train so that the name of Jesus could now spread into the mountain villages of the Sierra both north and south.

CHAPTER 20
LIKE A SCENE FROM THE BOOK OF ACTS

The west coast of Mexico can be described as mountains meeting the sea. They connect the Andes of South America to the Rockies of North America. There are tracts of flat land that separate the waters from the foothills, and others where the waves crash against steep cliffs. Acapulco nestles around a flat bay area encircled by a portion of the Sierra Madre del Sur. The narrow beaches of the Costa Chica stretch to the south, and of the Costa Grande to the north.

Now that Gustavo worked with the mission full-time, we alternated between the two areas. Gustavo had many contacts in the mountains to the south, and I had some from my work with Pastor Lacko in the north. The programs would run late because the men would be working the fields late, coming home expecting a meal before or after a program. So, oftentimes, we ran late and stayed overnight, not because we were very far away, but because the roads were difficult or dangerous at night.

Like a Scene From the Book of Acts

Spending a night in a mountain village is an experience in itself. Occasionally, there might be electricity, perhaps one lone light bulb illuminating an entire home. More often than not there's not. People will gather on porches in the darkened evenings with candles talking in hushed tones. When returning to their homes, they carry no flashlights to guide them along the narrow trails between the huts. I did.

In one place we stayed, there was a double bed. They insisted that I sleep on this, though two others joined me and we slept across the bed, legs dangling. The rest of the group spread out on quilts on the floor. Shortly after we turned in, someone jumped up screaming some not so nice Spanish words. They had lain on a scorpion.

One time, I slept on a quilt on the floor with two donkeys in the room. I was told if I made a little noise, the donkeys were smart enough not to step on me. Around 3:00 in the morning a rooster entered the room and crowed right in my ear. I instinctively batted it away and it ran out squawking, waking up dogs that began barking and the donkeys which began braying. Well, this woke up other dogs and donkeys in the village that took up the chorus. Saul just started singing. He figured since I had woken up the entire village and the animals were praising God, we might as well, too.

Another time, I slept near a barrel of corn. The cockroaches were plentiful. You really only needed to make sure you kept them out of your mouth unless you had a jar of Nutella nearby to go along with them.

The real danger in traveling the roads at night is the cartels. Most of the villages are controlled by the cartels, so we needed to get permission to visit, either through someone of influence in the area or directly dealing with the cartel. Without that permission, traveling at night would not be wise. Once, one of our young evangelists got over exuberant and preached at one of the men about how bad drugs were and they would do better to work as we were. Needless to say, this was not a good approach, as we were not allowed in that place.

In actuality, the cartels are not only feared, but, in ways, respected in the mountains. They provide work and pay well for the use of their land to grow marijuana. They assist the people more than the government by constructing buildings for the village, including churches, and helping with food when needed. Not that there is a lot of need for food. Most of their supply is grown on the land; and though it might lack in variation, it is generally plentiful. The people have a respect for this beautiful land.

One time, we had received permission to do a puppet show in a village, one of the men of the council that gave us permission took me aside and sarcastically asked, "Are you going to do anything helpful for the people other than preach at them?"

It knocked me for a loop. I began to realize that this is how people look at Christians. We come with our programs and our Bibles, we gather a crowd and build buildings and preach to the people; yet the village sees no real benefit to our presence.

We learned to assess situations in each area more carefully. Did we need to bring cooking essentials, like oils? Were blankets needed in the cold winter months? Though the temperatures only go down into the sixties, this is quite cold compared to the extreme heat of the rest of the year. So, what tangible ways could we express the love of Christ?

Around this time, we began to pay Gustavo about 3000 pesos ($300) for his full-time service; and I began to realize that I was slowing down the spread of the Gospel in the mountains.

The work generally only happened when all three of us went together. But more opportunities opened up for Sammy in the greater Acapulco area. Gustavo's and his wife's family connections in the mountains prevented him from being in two places at once. We decided they would work wherever God opened up for them regardless if I could go or not.

This left me with days alone to pray for them wherever they may be working. And I realized that my role was about to change again.

After being told by three different people that the perception of Christians by outsiders was that we went to church, meetings, and studied the Bible a lot, but they saw little or no effect upon the area in which they lived or worshipped. That got me thinking. How

Like a Scene From the Book of Acts

much of what I knew of God and the Bible translated into actual acts of love and sacrifice for others in the name of Jesus?

I put together a series of Bible teachings for small groups. The first half of the session consisted of two half hour studies; the first, would be basic Christian doctrine, the second covered practical applications like healing prayer or serving others. The remainder of the session, everyone would form groups of two or three and be sent into the streets to practice what they learned.

We started one such group in the godless town of Ayutla. There was a small church building here and we had done some work in the surrounding villages. The three-hour drive from Acapulco was so rough the skin on my elbow got tore off from bouncing on the armrest.

Christians from the mountains had been invited to attend this study, and we were pleasantly surprised to see close to 60 people crammed into the small building. The scent of human sweat in close proximity was lost in the intensity of concentration on the Word of God being taught by the pastors on our team. After the first two teachings were finished, we broke for lunch.

Upon their return, joyfully expecting more teaching, they were told to break up into groups of 2 or 3.

"What we're going to do now, is to go out into the streets and share what Christ has taught us and pray with people."

Joy turned to fear, anticipation to apprehension. Everyone looked around at each other, talking in hushed tones.

"Meet with people in their yard, ask if you can pray for them. Ask them their needs—are any sick? Be alert for signs of hunger. Be slow to speak. Listen, listen carefully. Build a relationship. Then pray, if they want to, specifically for their needs."

You could feel the uncertainty in the room. Everyone was hesitant to leave, but the leaders took charge and shepherded the groups into the street, and they headed off in different directions.

I stayed behind. I did not want to be the one they looked to for guidance, though I needed to convince a couple of the groups that this would not be painful. Joy crept into my heart as I looked up and down the little trails and dirt streets. People praying with women on porches, praying with men at their front door, laying hands and praying with people in the middle of the road.

Suddenly, one of the team members ran to me, eyes wide, arms waving. "Señor Jay, come quick!"

I ran with him as quickly as I could over fences, past donkeys and dogs and chickens, into a little darkened house. It took a bit for my eyes to adjust as I was led into the tiny bedroom. On a handmade quilt on the floor lay a woman, her family gathered around with worried faces. The lady was unable to get up and was experiencing severe abdominal pain. My first thoughts were "What could be wrong with her? Does she need medical attention?" But there are no doctors or hospitals for miles. They feared she would die.

We anointed her with oil. The three ladies who had come to me fervently prayed. Their apprehensions had disappeared. "¿Conces a Jesús?" asking about her relationship with God. They continued to pray and share the Gospel with her for almost an hour.

As I stepped out of the crowded room to get some air, someone grabbed my arm. "Come and see!" There on that old quilt sat the woman, upright and smiling. Two of the ladies helped her to her feet. Awed silence filled the room.

We had told the group to return to the church after an hour, but two hours had passed and only a few had made it back. And then they slowly started returning, not with faces of fear and trepidation but of joy and excitement. Through much clapping of hands and shouts of praise, everyone tried to tell their stories at once.

After finally getting the group seated, they came up one by one to tell of the many wonderful things God had done that day. This continued for some time as they could not stop praising God! They now knew that God could use them right there, all they needed do was just go.

We use this model all over the mountains now, as well as within Acapulco. Sammy has done a fantastic job with these small groups. He has also organized the teenagers at the base church in Palenque to regularly go into the streets; these young people find this more exciting than just a teen outing at the beach. This church has a strong foundation and continues to affect their area. It's not about just coming to church for them; it's about coming as the church to go out and serve as Christ served and to observe first-hand God working in the hearts of people through them.

CHAPTER 21
CHURCH IN A ROCK

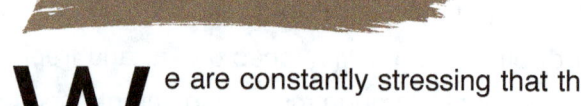

We are constantly stressing that the church is not just a place to come to learn, but to practice what we learn. Praying in the streets and throughout the community occurs weekly and each small group looks for ways to fill needs within their neighborhood.

To be seen by the entire community, one Sunday a month they organize a parade. Colorful signs and drawings proclaim Jesus. Children ride bicycles down the street, streamers fluttering in the breeze and little horns beeping. Much singing and dancing weaves its way through the area of ministry. Some walk along handing out flyers declaring the way of salvation with contact information for prayer or other needs.

I must tell you about another little church that Gustavo helped nurture with a wonderful saint of God, Rosa, a big woman with a heart and soul for Jesus and people to match. Rosa, her husband, and children needed a place to live, so ten years ago they carved out a large room in the side of the mountain near downtown Acapulco. With hammer and chisel they continued carving—a small bathroom, a pool that collects water, a bedroom, and a larger

room that doubles as kitchen and meeting room for her Bible study she started some years ago.

White plastic chairs used for a 20-minute Bible study and time of worship are put aside and folding tables are brought out for a meal cooked by Rosa. Afterwards, two by two, everyone takes to the street to pray with people and give out food. Within an hour or so, they return to share testimony of what God has done. This makes for very exciting church as they see the miracles of God on a weekly basis.

To this day, these small groups continue to grow and become a vital part of the churches. Some modifications are made to the

programs for the groups in the mountains. The men rise early to go up with their donkeys to the fields or to tend sheep and goats all day. Programs are scheduled on weekends to accommodate and minister to these men.

Sammy and Gustavo, sometimes together, sometimes separately, organized groups of loyal new churches in the mountains, teaching them basic doctrine and identifying those with gifts to teach and lead. My work now was that of advisor and encourager. I helped set the teaching agenda, but they had to make modifications to adapt to mountain village lifestyle and culture. Gustavo and his wife are absolutely invaluable with this, both coming from mountain villages.

We still have the same two vehicles we've been using for some time, the 2002 Ford Escape and a little '98 Ford truck. One of the miracles of Acapulco is that these vehicles are still running! Most of the parts have been replaced from hard driving on the mountain roads, not to mention the extremely rough city roads. In

America, mountain roads tend to snake and curve making for a more gradual climb. Most of the time here it's a straight shot to the top, engine whining in the high altitude. We'd have to stop for an hour or so to let the engine cool. Other places the road was just a donkey trail, rock face less than a foot out the window, steep drop-off to other side less than a foot away from the tires gripping the ground. How these vehicles continued to run in these conditions is truly of God. We do pray for the Lord to supply more reliable transportation soon.

So, the work had expanded remarkably: growth in numbers, growth in maturity. And I began to sense yet another change in my life was soon to take place.

CHAPTER 22
TIME TO LEAVE

I continued to teach Sammy and Gustavo hermeneutics, biblical interpretation, and Sammy and Pamela basic English. We did this about three days a week and they would bring their children with them, who would sit and watch cartoons while we studied. Why were the children not in school? Because, for various reasons, the schools are hardly open. When they are open it may be for 3 or 4 days, 4 hours a day.

Generally, the schools are in older buildings and have no regular janitor; therefore, the children are required to help with clean-up. There are no lunches or lunch programs. The Mexican school system is under the total control of the teacher's union. Regular protests for more money block roads for hours. There are numerous holidays for days off. And to top it off, on a regular basis, kidnappers prowl the schools looking for children whose parents have a bit of money. When the teachers get wind of it, they just don't show up. The children could arrive to find a sign on the door stating "No school until…"

For Sammy's and Gustavo's education, I stressed that a good message took hours of hard work and should be based on the Bible, not how we feel or what impresses us. I found they were trying to imitate televangelists they had access to.

As they implemented this teaching, the church grew in maturity in Palenque and the outskirts of Acapulco, and in the mountain churches. I would go with Gustavo into the mountains for one or two days, then spend the weekend with Sammy. Watching these churches grow, I began to realize that I wasn't really needed. Being freed to follow God's leading instead of checking in with me,

growth came fast and smooth under their direction and leading.

Over a period of about two months, it was impressed on my heart that I could be more useful in the States raising funds. I re-

Time to Leave

turned for three weeks to find a place to live. My wife and I had not yet reunited. After much looking, I found an affordable townhouse in Castlewood and reserved it for one month after. I returned to Mexico to attend to the details of leaving Mexico full-time.

The cable company didn't want to cut off the cable. It took eight trips to the local and downtown offices—including the morning I left and Sammy double-checking that afternoon—to get it done. Bribes are a way of life here, so a 100 pesos bribe to the meter reader got the electricity immediately cut.

Though there were plenty of tears of sadness, it was clear to me that they accepted this as my time to leave. We arranged for Skype meetings and a promise to return once or twice a year for a conference.

I took the 6½ hour bus trip to Mexico City to spend a couple of days with my dear friends in the Jewish community before returning to Charleston, SC. One of my great joys when I got back was being able to drive on good roads where people actually stop for red lights and stop signs.

CHAPTER 23
THOUGHTS ON THE BUS

Taking the bus to Mexico City instead of flying out from Acapulco to connect a flight to the States saved me almost $400; a senior discount for the bus plus taxi fares costs less than $20 US. It also makes for a more adventurous trip. Once, on the way to Mexico City, the brakes went out on the mountain road. Fortunately, there was a runaway truck ramp, a sandy incline for just such emergencies. Several ladies huddled under the shade of a nearby tree while we waited a couple of hours in the heat for a replacement bus. This gave me opportunity to share the Lord with them. Another time, returning to Acapulco this time, the bus had a flat tire. The driver limped it into a restaurant parking lot to fix it, while we sat at a large, round table in the non-air-conditioned restaurant. I did meet another Christian at that time, forming another contact.

I thought of these experiences as the bus rolled out of Acapulco. Climbing the mountain road, I could see down into the val-

Thoughts on the Bus

ley. I could see small clearings and groups of dwellings where we had spent so much time working and ministering and building relationships. Many feelings flooded my soul as many tears flowed down my cheeks.

Moving beyond the capital city of Chilpancingo, moving closer to Mexico City, I thought of my Jewish friends, Jessica and Moses de Ida, that I would be staying with for a couple of days before continuing on. We met at the pool at the condominium overlooking Acapulco Bay. At the time, these were the only English-speaking people I knew.

As our friendship grew, they began to travel with us on some of the mountain trips and fell in love with what we were doing for the people, giving hope and meeting needs. Though they have yet to accept the gospel, they respect it, and we all agree that our motivation to help people is because of God's love for us. I have spent many Shabbat dinners with them and have come to know their entire family. I have even been to a funeral that lasted seven days for a member of the family. Jessica and Moses formed a charitable group for people to donate clothes and toys and household items, which are stored in great quantity in a room of their house. These items are brought to Acapulco for the single mothers and widows to sell on the street to earn money. I learned a lot about the Lord's Supper by participating in Passover, a celebration of deliverance, with them. There is more to it than just eating bread and drinking wine. There are dinners and celebrations with the immediate family and extended family, with the church family, as well as a time of recognition of their oneness with brothers and sisters around the world. I began thinking about inviting them to the States once I got re-established.

The bus pulled into Mexico City, but my journey was not over. I had a two-hour taxi ride to their home. I spent a couple of days visiting with Jessica and Moses before flying back to South Carolina. It was a hectic week and a half setting up the apartment, buying furniture, and settling in. I stayed in almost daily contact with Sammy and Gustavo and even arranged for a return trip in about three months.

CHAPTER 24
FIRST TRIP BACK: HEAL THE SICK, CAST OUT DEVILS

It took a few weeks to settle back into the States. The roads seemed smoother than what I had become accustomed to. I began to go to the gym again—and it was air conditioned, an unheard-of luxury in Acapulco. I took quiet walks on clean beaches; the beaches of Mexico were more like flea markets, covered with huts that were expensive to rent and vendors constantly approaching you, selling food and trinkets. Not a restful experience. The team in Mexico and I stayed in touch 3 to 5 times a week via Skype, email, or phone.

After about three months, I received a call from a trusted friend, a leader in the Presbyterian Church in Acapulco and a man with the gift of discernment. We worked many times together building a church and with Mission Acapulco. He was concerned that some unscriptural practices were being held in some of the newer churches regarding healing; practices they learned from watching television evangelists.

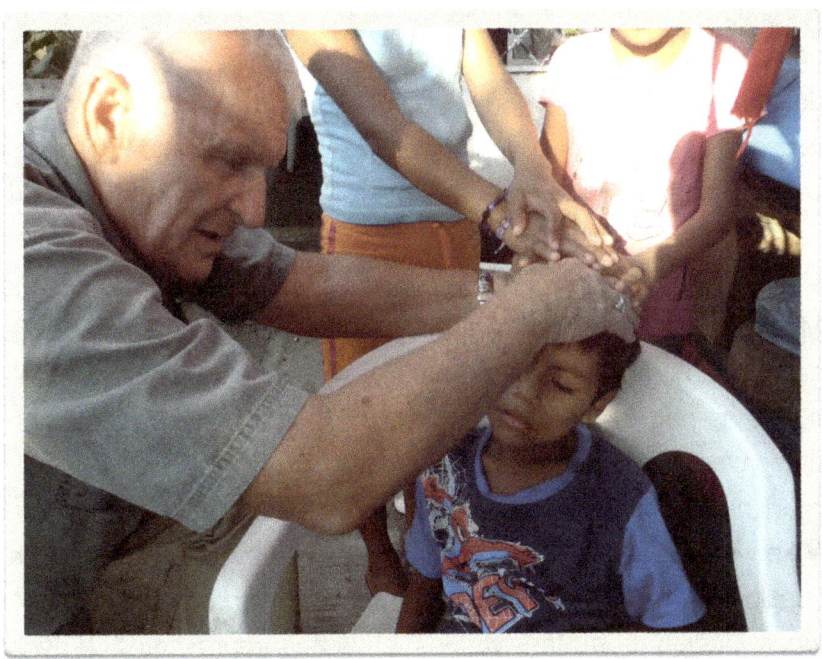

While in Mexico, I saw many miracles of healing. I remember once a man who had not walked for several years after an accident came to see us in a wheelchair for prayer and went away walking. I tried to memorize the words I said, recalling the steps I took to duplicate the experience; but it didn't work, though the opportunity occurred again and again. The fact is, what I said or what I did made little or no difference. It's God's work! I have actually seen more healings take place as people pray for one another than when one person prays in a public setting. I think it's because we tend to give glory to one praying instead of to God who does the healing. And God does not do miracles to show off,

He has specific purposes—like to get the attention of the whole family or village or to open doors to places that are closed by the cartels or witchcraft.

I spoke with Sammy about what my friend had relayed to me and after much discussion decided to put together a training series on healing ministry. The Lord laid on my heart to call Dr. Bruce Quinlan, a dear friend and accountability partner for many years, who holds a doctorate in prayer counseling and has a private practice. Bruce put me in touch with Dr. Francis and Judith McNutt from Healing Prayer Ministries in Jacksonville, FL and Michael Evans in Bakersfield, CA, whose books and teachings have been translated into Spanish. We would use one of his books as part of the training. After much prayer and discussion, dates were set, and a format determined.

The attendance far exceeded our expectations. Bruce and Mike would teach 30 minutes each, followed by 15 minutes of discussion or practical application with 15 minute breaks between. At lunch, ladies from the various churches represented brought beans and tacos and we purchased extra food. This is typical of all of our meetings and what is leftover is sold afterward to benefit those in need.

The evening service was 45 minutes of solid biblical teaching. Both Bruce and Mike were clear that though some in the church certainly have the gift of healing, God can and will use anyone—it's not dependent on man's ability, but God's will. Afterward, time was given for anyone who wanted healing prayer and for anyone who felt they wanted to pray for others to come forward.

There was no soft music, no special lighting or smoke machines, or anything to arouse or distract or build emotion. Occasionally, quiet speaking or singing in tongues could be heard.

Some of this was new to me. My experience of praying for the sick in church would be merely to anoint them with oil (biblical), lay hands (biblical), and say a quick prayer and move on. Here, we used oil and laid on hands, but instead of doing all the talking, we asked, we listened, we waited. In teams of two, one person spoke with the sick, while the other observed and prayed in support. We looked for signs of healing—shaking, heat, anything indicating a change. If after a time there was no change, we prayed God's blessing over them and went to the next person. No microphones, no show.

There were two or three people who seemed to be possessed. These were people in real need asking for prayer, but when the name of Jesus was spoken, they reacted violently. This scared me; I was afraid it could get out of hand. But Mike calmly intervened, and in a stern, yet quiet voice told the person to sit down and be quiet in the name of Jesus. Immediately the person sat down and was quiet. Mike explained that God has the power over Satan, and we don't back down.

Many miracles happened that day, including lives given to Christ. God is still healing today—body and spirit. All needs to be focused on Jesus, as it is too easy to get caught up in the praises and accolades of men. This is dangerous because Satan is always ready to destroy the ministry of God. As a hedge against the showmanship of televangelists, all of our contacts in Mexico have access to Mike Evans books.

The team left and we visited a few places where we were working with other churches before taking a much needed day off. And then Sammy got a phone call. A lady who had taken her daughter to one of the services needed our help. After the service, her daughter became deranged and violent.

First Trip Back: Heal the Sick, Cast Out Devils

Before first light, we picked up one of the elders of the church in Palenque and Gustavo and Raquel. As our tires crunched up the little gravel trail, Gustavo explained that they felt she had been affected by witchcraft.

We arrived at the little cement block house surrounded by a broken fence and went in past a small reservoir of water for washing, common for homes in the area. As our eyes adjusted to the dim light of the living room, we saw the young girl, about 13, sitting on a little chair in a stupor. I approached, placed my hand on her shoulder, and began to pray in the name of Jesus. At the name of Jesus she thrust my hand away.

The Spirit moved me to have Raquel, an elder, and another pray for her as I stepped aside. The girl's face remained expressionless. They continued in prayer for about 15-20 minutes when she began to convulse and resist them.

Sammy motioned to me to follow him outside. I sat in a broken chair and Sammy sat on a boulder just outside the door. And we prayed. We prayed for at least 30 minutes before going back inside. The girl sat on a stone ledge now. A lady in a red dress we hadn't seen before and assumed was a friend stood nearby. We began to pray again and she left immediately, rapidly running across the road.

The three continued in fervent prayer. The girl coughed violently. Spit and phlegm mixed with her tears fell to the dirt floor pooling with the tears of those praying.

Sammy and I once again went outside to pray. I bowed my head. Sammy paced, praying in tongues. He stopped by a gatepost and motioned for me to bring him a heavy stick laying near my feet. Digging around the post with the stick, he finally exposed the top of a mason jar. Lifting the jar out of the ground, we saw that it was filled with a thick, red substance. Stuffed inside were some feminine products, a pair of panties, and a picture of Jesus with the head cut off. Sammy smashed the jar and put everything in a pile next to the fire pit. Then he began to pace and pray in the Spirit again. By the leading of the Holy Ghost he found two more mason jars filled with similar objects.

We went back inside to inform the others of what we found. We then decided to check her room as well. The room contained a broken-down chest of drawers, two single beds, and a mattress. We searched the floor for loose dirt and checked the drawers and mattresses. We found a couple of items that bore significance and took them to the pile outside. Paying a neighbor a few pesos for a quart of gasoline, we set the pile ablaze. Someone also asked for salt, as they had correctly read in the Old Testament that salt was used to purify a residence. So, we took a handful of salt and sprinkled it throughout the house.

The young girl stood calmly and quietly standing in the kitchen clutching a Bible. Raquel and the girl's mother led her to the front room and washed her from the water in the reservoir. They brought her outside into the late morning sun and I could see a little smile on her face as Raquel held her and brushed her hair, surrounding her with the love of Jesus. We sang a few praise songs and left. I heard that she was back in church and doing quite well. The witch did not try to visit the house again.

I often think what would have happened to her here in our country. I suspect she would have been taken to see a counselor or psychiatrist, and in her condition, committed to an institution. It makes me wonder if we miss opportunities or lack the faith, as I did, to see demon possession as the root of a problem, a problem that can only be cast out by faith and prayer.

CHAPTER 25
ANOTHER RETURN TRIP: BACK TO THE MOUNTAINS

Approximately four months later, I returned for a two-week visit. I did not make return visits just for the sake of making a trip. Sammy and I talked two or three times a week. He would share with me what he was working on and, in this case, that he wanted to expand the small groups ministry. He was working with Saul again, who had new areas in the Sierra Madre that he wanted help with from Mission Acapulco. Since I have many friends in those mountains, Sammy felt it would be good for me to come with them.

Though my personal finances were a struggle at the time, God has always made a way for my travels, either by help from our small board giving sacrificially or by a blessing in my small insurance business.

When I arrived, Sammy showed me the schedule of activities (Sammy always had a schedule of activities). It was scary. Every day crammed from early morning to late at night. Of course, a lot of time would be spent traveling. These intense itineraries would take their toll on me physically and mentally, but God would always see me through.

I shared our vision about small groups with a large group of young people. We are so blessed that God has brought so many young people into the church. The danger, though, with groups of young people is that you do as much teaching as you can with an excessive amount of entertainment to keep them interested. Young people dream dreams, and when they are born again God wants to use their enthusiasm and energy to do His work. So, of course, there were times we would get them together to eat or an occasional day at the beach; but mostly, we helped train them to help others as a group and to pray with people in the streets.

After a couple of teachings, they dispersed into the streets with signs saying, "Rezaremos por ti, solo pide." (We will pray for you, just ask.) The tiny apartments of Palenque are hot. People sat outside on little plastic chairs on their 10' x 10' patch of dirt in front of the buildings. These teenagers boldly made sure to ask everyone sitting out that evening if they wanted prayer. And many did. They also set up a sign and a couple of chairs on the street corners and people would come to them for prayer. Though some adults went with them, they were not as bold about their faith. These young people are fearless and are a major catalyst for so much growth in this church.

So, of course we wanted to transfer this enthusiasm for the Lord Jesus into as many areas as possible. It is amazing to see this ministry grow, even in the mountains. Their enthusiasm en-

courages the older generation to also be vocal about sharing their faith.

    I also had privilege of teaching at a new church in Casitas. This is near Palenque, but again, because of the difficulty of the terrain and the lack of transportation, seems so much further. The church has a very good young pastor and his wife and a core of about 20 people. We trained them to work in the streets and they were very interested in partnering with Mission Acapulco in other ways. We needed a new treasurer because the previous treasurer had become too busy and traveled; therefore, it was difficult to find him when money was needed for gas money or car repairs. This young pastor consented to take on this responsibility, but a month after I left, he decided he could do it no longer. Sammy then had the responsibility of leading the mission, pastoring a church, and now handling the money. We knew that was not healthy, but God would deal with this on the next trip.

    Saul made a contact in the small village of Petalis, a good ways into the Sierra Madre, requiring a long, hard day to get there and other places he wished us to see. Pastor Lacko told me some time before that this was a difficult place for any Christian activity, though they had success in other nearby villages. But God put it on my heart that we had to go there.

Again, I found myself on donkey trails that no vehicle had business to traverse. Saul drove, while Sammy, Pamela, and I hung on for dear life and prayed. We stopped in many little places along the way but made no meaningful contacts. It was getting late, and even though it meant going down the rocky, sandy trail in the dark, something we avoided in the past because of the danger of carjacking and robbery, I felt in my spirit we must continue.

We took a little side trail, and after a tortuous mile of dodging rocks and holes, we started seeing small mudbrick homes and a few cement block buildings. We found Petalis.

Every village, no matter how small, has a central court built by the government. There's a basketball hoop or soccer nets and most have a covering. These areas are used by the politicians to give speeches and hand out food to buy votes. We use them with the permission from the village leaders to perform our programs. The road ended at the central court of Petalis.

As we got out of the car to stretch and look around, God directed my gaze to a house across the street. I began to move toward it and my steps quickened, as though God were nudging me along. I got to the covered walkway and asked loudly if anyone was there. A lady came out and I explained that we wanted to use central court to do a puppet show for the village. It didn't take long for us both to know we were brother and sister in Christ. She and her husband and two daughters were the only Christians in the village. One daughter was actually at Bible school in Tulsa, OK, married, and working in a Spanish community. As darkness was coming on and we needed to leave, we arranged to return and do the puppet show and they would advertise it.

The next week, as we were preparing to go, Sammy told us of a message he had received the night before. He was told that we would be in grave danger because of one of the workers, a minister of the Assemblies of God of Mexico, going with us. Supposedly, he was accused of having a baby with a member of a cartel family. After much prayer, we decided that either Sammy or I go, not both, in case of trouble. It would be me, Gustavo and his wife, and a puppet team of three.

We loaded the Blazer and Sammy put out the word that the accused pastor would not be with us. We heard nothing, but we also did not receive any more threats, so we went and performed the program. This led to a small group church led by the lady we first met. Because of its isolation and difficulty to get to during the monsoon periods, we have only been able to help with some occasional supplies and teaching materials.

This also taught us an important lesson to be careful about who works with us. Dr. David Monterey of the Presbyterian Church spent time with us going over a vetting process they use for determining elders.

Before I left, I spent some time visiting small Assemblies of God churches on the old road to Mexico City. We did programs for these struggling churches and tried to help them grow any way we could. We realize as a part of the denomination that they would never really become a part of Mission Acapulco, but they welcome our help and they have become dear friends to this day.

Upon my return to the States, it took me about 34 days to rest and fully recover physically.

CHAPTER 26
THIRD TRIP BACK: LEADERSHIP TRAINING

Many conversations concerning the attitude of much of the Mexican church about leadership—they are very big on their titles—lead to my third trip back. Customarily, as soon as a person comes to church, they are immediately given something to do. This is good, but it has to come with a title. Also, the ministers and one or two elders make all of the decisions for the church and are expected to do any and all evangelism. This is due to the pastors generally having more education, especially in the mountains. So, we put together a two-hour teaching on church leadership with time after for discussion.

Early the next morning, Gustavo and I drove 2½ hours up into the mountains to meet with 12 area pastors. We gathered around two long tables sitting on old, cracked plastic chairs reviewing the training and refining the locations to hold the session. Outside, four ladies and a teenager prepared tortillas and chopped peppers for salsa. Once the dates and times for each location were set, we

Third Trip Back: Leadership Training

ate tortillas and chili and lots of beans. Afterward, as I said goodbyes to the others, Gustavo spoke with one of the pastors off to the side.

We got in the truck to begin the long ride back down the mountain and as I settled in, Gustavo explained that one of the pastors was dedicating a new church building. He asked that we participate and would I give a message.

We got there close to dark and already a lot of very excited people had arrived. There was an hour before the service, so I laid in a hammock at the house next to the church to rest and pray that God would give me the words to bless the pastor at this new church.

As this was an Assemblies of God, as is their custom, the men sat on one side and the women on the other. Normally, the children would have a separate class, but tonight they sat with

Third Trip Back: Leadership Training

their mothers. We were led outside, where Gustavo performed a wonderful service anointing the outer archway and then the entry door with oil. I had no interpreter, but God undertook as I delivered a message, then laid hands on the new pastor. A group of young people were presented. I was told that this was a new puppet ministry that would work in the surrounding area. I laid hands on them and as I prayed we were all overwhelmed with tears of joy.

We finally returned to Acapulco sometime after midnight because, of course, we ate again; this time a bit of chicken with a red-hot mole, and, of course, tortillas.

The next morning, we set out for Atoyac, a city at the base of the Sierra Mountains two hours to the north. The road is not bad going until you get to the neighborhood of the church where it's just dirt and rocks. I once visited this church, and the services ran

Third Trip Back: Leadership Training

so late I ended up sleeping on the roof for about three hours before the roosters woke me up.

The meeting was well received. The title of the lecture was "The Men That God Uses". We detailed the characteristics of over 20 people in the Bible and showed that, in spite of our weakness-

es and shortcomings, all of us can be and must allow ourselves to be used of God for His purposes and His glory.

Oftentimes in the mountains we slept on dirt floors; occasionally, a mattress might be available. Hammocks are great for me to sleep in for about 4 or 5 hours before I need to get up, stretch, and turn over. Tonight, I slept on a cement floor. Getting older, this becomes more difficult, as every little rock or uneven spot on the floor seems to find my hip; so, I turn to find another spot with the other hip, then the back and shoulders or tailbone. Sleep is in small bits at a time.

Third Trip Back: Leadership Training

The following morning, we headed to a place called St. Christopher, another steep ride up the mountains on decent roads until the last 20 km. Here, the main crop is coffee and bananas, which are all over. The whole area of Atoyac is known for its coffee and I take back as much as customs will allow.

We were greeted warmly. We walked about a half mile up and down hills to a little church built of palm boards. Palm boards deteriorate rapidly, so cracks of 1 to 3 inches were everywhere ventilating the building. Thin boards were nailed to the palm tree stumps as makeshift pews, seating maybe 50 people. Some neighboring pastors arrived on motorbikes and 4-wheelers. The pastor lived in a little house of mud bricks behind the church and raised goats and chickens.

It was hot, but people's ears were open. Sammy and Gustavo knew the material well, each doing their part, and then a time of prayer and commitment.

Afterwards, we walked down a short steep hill to the pastor's house and were served a meal of rice, chicken and broth with tortillas as utensils.

We left and returned to our cars where a lady had prepared another meal of equal size. This made for a very long day.

The next day we went early to the house of Pastor Israel. He and his wife work in the coffee industry, roasting, grinding, and selling coffee. They seldom use a coffeemaker, but simply boil the grounds, then strain it through cheesecloth into a cup. This is the smoothest coffee I've ever had, not a hint of bitterness. We followed him to another mountain church with just a few people.

We arrived at the house of one of the families next to the central court where they had setup about 75 rented or borrowed chairs. Immediately, Sammy and Gustavo went separate ways with flyers telling people about a free program and movie that

Third Trip Back: Leadership Training

night. I walked along the hard trail and a nice man brought me a hand-carved cane and gave it to me. He said he makes several a week to sell. I was most grateful for it.

A sheet stretched from the basketball backboard to the nearby fence. A sheet works well so that shy people on the other side of the street can watch from their porches. We showed the movie "Facing the Giants" (in Spanish). The chairs filled quickly. Many sat behind a low cement wall so they couldn't be seen. This town, as many are, was controlled by the cartel and this was the first time a program had been done there. Sammy and Israel gave the altar call after the movie and several came forward.

After the altar call, I was quite tired and ready to go. I stood by the Ford Escape as it was being loaded, when I was summoned to meet two men, both teary eyed and looking like they hadn't slept in a week.

"Tenemos sangre en nuestras manon. Trabajamos con el extorsionista."

They confessed they had been working with an extortionist and had blood on their hands. Pastor Israel was called over. After much prayer and showing them the way to Christ, they received the Lord Jesus. Sammy and I charged Pastor Israel to follow-up and help them. They actually left town to live with Pastor Israel in Atoyac.

If you'll recall, Sammy and Pamela still handled the money themselves, as they still could not find anyone to take the responsibility of treasurer. Sammy felt this improper, as it could cause distrust for anyone wanting to know how the money was spent. Neither are bookkeepers, although they are extremely careful with money. They had no ledger, only a box of receipts.

Two nights before we left, I called Dr. Monterey who met with us. We asked Sammy and Gustavo what had been done so far to get a new treasurer. They started to say they had asked a lot of people, when it dawned on them that they had not asked God to send a treasurer. After referring to Scripture, we all prayed earnestly and specifically for the Lord to supply a treasurer before I left.

The very next day, we received a call from someone who knew we were looking for a treasurer and suggested we call Hector Betancourt, a successful businessman with a restaurant on the waterfront. We called and he agreed to meet with us; whereupon we learned that he also treasured for Samaritan's Purse in Guerro. Though very busy—besides the restaurant and Samaritan's Purse, he pastors a church—he is very well organized and agreed to help and to keep a proper ledger. He speaks English well, making it easier to communicate with the treasurer in the States, and he continues to send monthly reports to the board here.

Again, we learned to first look to God in deep and fervent prayer believing that He will supply all our needs according to His riches in glory, which He promised in Philippians 4:19.

The next day we held a conference in an area just outside the Acapulco city limits, an area where the houses crowd up and are attached to one another and most are also business fronts with the living space in the back. The church, though attached to a house on each side, held 200 or more, very large for a Mexican church, and the church was close to full. Outside, ladies cooked tortillas and beans over a wood fire.

We taught two parts: first, the doctrinal basis that every Christian is a leader according to the gifts given to them by God; secondly, practical ways the various gifts could be used in the community in the name Christ. At the end of the service, many came forward asking that God empower them to use their gifts.

Third Trip Back: Leadership Training

As a general rule, Mexican people can be more emotional, and oftentimes, good speakers and preachers will take advantage of that to prove their ministry—the results are not lasting. In my teaching, I have learned to use nothing but Bible verses and sections, realizing the power of God is <u>His</u> Word, not mine.

The lasting impact of this trip became evident on subsequent trips, as God moved people to service, not necessarily in the church, but in the streets and in the workplace and with neighbors.

The last trip took us so high up the mountain I thought the Ford would explode, it whined so terribly. The center of this village was so beautiful. The residents paved the streets themselves with sacks of concrete they bought whenever they could afford, leveling it out with boards and a few trowels. It was fairly smooth and dust free.

Third Trip Back: Leadership Training

Canvases were tied to trees to keep off the sun. Sammy, Gustavo, and I gave the message of how God uses broken vessels to do His will. There was great response from this little group of 30 or so. Immediately after the service we paired up two by two and went out into the village to see what the needs were and to pray for people.

Everyone excitedly shared their stories when they returned, and this little outdoor church is growing. Sister Rosa, the lady who started the cave church in Acapulco is overseeing its growth.

Before leaving, we took the last afternoon to sit under a bamboo hut on the beach. We prayed that the messages bear fruit. We talked about the growth God had given in Palenque and especially in the mountains. I got to meet Alfredo and his wife, new to the work in another area of the mountains. Since the conferences, he became very inspired and there are close to 100 new Christians in that area. I believe all this is the direct answer to Capt. Brenton's prayers for Southwest Mexico.

And as the work continues to grow, I am once again impressed upon that I am only one piece of the puzzle—not less, not more—in God's plan for this area. Flying home, I reflected on how God uses broken vessels. Certainly, I am one. More than a few tears fell in total gratitude to my gracious God.

CHAPTER 27
FOOT WASHING: LEADERSHIP TRAINING PART II

It was assumed that I would make two trips a year—one in early spring, the other in late fall. These are the best times of the year to have access to the total ministry area. There were more than a few times while I lived there that I was trapped on the mountain during the rainy season, which starts about the middle of June to the end of September, unless there are hurricanes, which pose another threat. We might be doing a program and not have rain where we were, but maybe hear some thunder in the distance. Upon returning home, we might come across a river or stream we crossed going up, but now the water is rushing down, and we'd have to wait 7 or 8 hours for it to abate. Unless the river crosses a well-traveled area between major cities, there are no bridges. Some people living nearby might haul flat stones to make a bit of a roadbed to cross. Other months to avoid are the middle of September to late October and the entire month of May. The humidity and temperature during this time can be unbearable to anyone not used to it. So, most of my return trips are in March and April, and October and November.

The purpose of the trips is defined by the team in Mexico. They relay the needs and I formulate appropriate teaching. I do not get involved in the day-to-day planning or details of the program; the team has people that do that much better than myself. My role concerns the initiation of the teaching working jointly with the team. It's important they are involved so the people know the teaching comes from their leadership and not solely from me in the US, though I lived among them for over 10 years.

We are in daily communication before these trips, arranging schedules. I have to pray over these schedules because they pack them to the point that each day is full—12 to 15 hours with hard travel. I don't think they want to accept that my body is getting older. They relentlessly try to use every minute for ministry. Someday I would like to make a trip back just to visit friends—slowly.

At this time, they had noticed that in many of the newly founded churches and others we had built that there was a feeling that the pastor was extremely special and that many of the pastors took advantage of this. This was amazing because we thought we had dealt with this the last trip.

So, we determined to teach the doctrine that every believer is prophet, priest, and king. The first half of the session we'd teach that each of us in Christ are special, are appointed, and are anointed. The second part of the session would be a foot washing, teaching how this showed hospitality in Israel. Setting up about a dozen little plastic tubs of water at the front row, we encouraged the leaders and pastors to come and show their willingness to wash the feet of the members of their group, towels draped over their shoulder, kneeling down to wash their feet and pray. Then those who had their feet washed would take a turn washing other's feet. In most cases, everyone participated. In all gatherings, large and small, emotions flowed and tears fell in abundance as the Holy Spirit impressed this teaching deep into their spirits and ours as we felt our equality in Christ.

Because of the subtle persecution of Christians in Mexico by the government, these groups already feel a closeness to one another. The only churches to receive tax relief are those who have political connections. Tax collection in many areas is enforced more strictly against churches than most businesses. (I find it interesting that I have never heard the church being harassed by the extortionists.) I know that even the Catholic Church in Mexico has been stripped of power and property. Those that come to Christ band together in the churches, as do the Jewish people in their groups and synagogues. I believe this contributed greatly to the depth of feeling in both small and large venues.

Now the team had received a request from a missionary who had attended one of the services to go to the city of Morrelles. This county-sized area is on the western edge of Mexico City. I think Sammy and I both had visions that perhaps God would expand our ministry further out from Acapulco, so we prayed and planned for this long trip. I have often prided myself on my discernment, the man seemed genuine, but I was about to receive a lesson.

We traveled the old road, winding and steep with not a few potholes, to avoid the toll road with its many toll booths as much as possible; though, to save time, we traveled it some. Having left early in the morning, we arrived later in the day to perform the first service, the doctrinal teaching, that evening. When we returned

Foot Washing: Leadership Training Part II

late to the home we were staying in, several of us, including 1 or 2 English-speakers, gathered around the table and talked until early morning.

The next day, Saturday, we all gathered again for the foot washing, about 75 total, many related, most leaders from surrounding churches that had formed an alliance. Everyone came

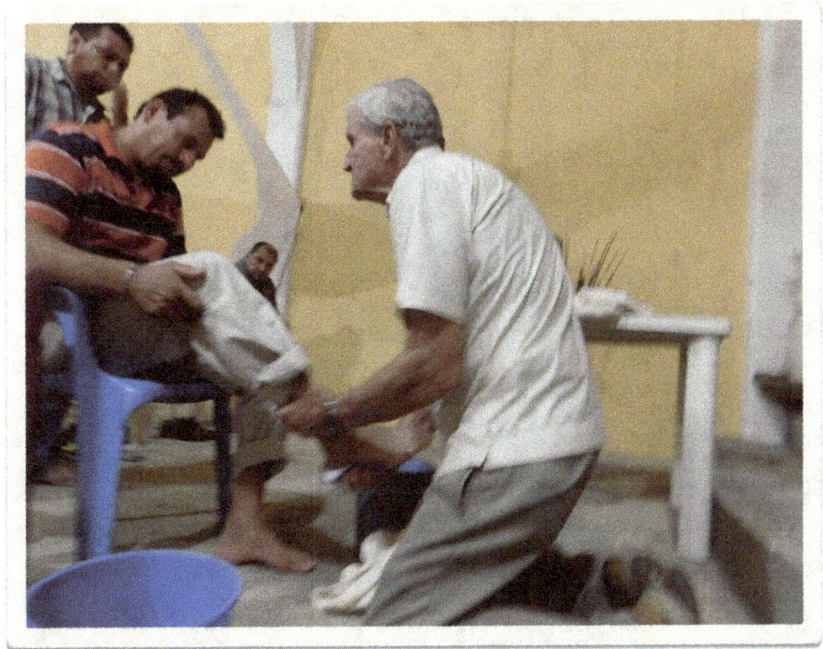

forward to do the foot washing, except for seven pastors who sat in a row with their arms crossed, neither smiling nor frowning, only observing. Sammy, being a bit aggravated with the situation, spoke with them and found that they felt it beneath their dignity to wash the feet of others.

Foot Washing: Leadership Training Part II

Afterward, while eating tortillas and chicken broth, I heard the confusion of the people at the actions of these leaders. The message had been diminished. I felt let down.

When it was time to leave, a couple of people wanted us to go see where they wanted to build a home for children. It turned out to be a long way off, and when we got there, they began telling us how we could help them by being a major supporter and purchase the land and buildings. They had no interest in being a part of Mission Acapulco. We had this problem frequently in the early days of the ministry. Our purpose is to spread the Gospel, not to be a bank ATM. As Gustavo has explained quite well to many churches, when people are saved and the church grows, God will supply those needs; it is not what we do.

I met with my Jewish friends who took me to Mexico City for a couple days before returning to the States. I thought about the trip to Morelles being nothing but trouble—the expense of the trip, the wear and tear on the vehicles, the discouragement. Our pride and desire for expansion clouded our discernment. Proverbs 3:5-7a, "Trust in the Lord with all your heart, and lean not on your own understanding; in all your ways acknowledge Him, and He shall direct your paths. <u>Do not be wise in your own eyes.</u>" I can only trust that God used the messages, and that people learned their worth and value to God apart from official titles. We trust that God <u>will</u> use it for good and the good of His kingdom.

CHAPTER 28
LOOKING FOR JOSHUA

For the past 2 or 3 years, I have had trouble with neuropathy in my feet—a numbness and burning that affects my balance. I do fine in the US but find it more difficult to walk up and down the little mountain trails, climbing over rocks, or even navigating the steps up to the church in Palenque. So, returning, I realized I needed to find someone to replace me.

Should it be one person, bilingual, with ministry experience and able to travel? Maybe a couple, a bilingual husband and wife team capable of teaching? Perhaps a church with not just financial resources, but teaching resources? Would I be able to pass it on and release the vision into new hands without trying to maintain control? These questions permeated my prayers. Sammy and Pamela and all the others—these are my children. But I knew it was time to step aside.

And there were so many other blessings and spiritual children that God gave me there. A top-tier tennis coach who became born again and I was able to nurture him in the faith. The young pilot who stayed with me while he trained at the Acapulco airport—he and two of his friends became Christians. His mother, an artist and writer living in Mexico City would visit and I had the honor of baptizing them both in the ocean. The ball boys and caddies at the Mayan Palace, the tourists, the wealthy businessmen—whom all I befriended and they in turn befriended Jesus.

After about a month, my heart was burdened, so I wrote a list of possible contacts and started making calls. But as soon as they learned I was looking for more than to just share pictures of my experiences, I was put off. Call after call after call the same: not interested.

I was frustrated. I was impatient. I was irreverent. "Why is this taking so long, Lord? Why?"

I knew in my heart this was His work, not mine, and that He had a plan. *Dios siempre tiene un plan.* I wearied of waiting, but knew I needed to continue.

I finally received some invitations to small church groups. I asked, but no. I spoke at various Spanish groups, but they were either already helping churches and families in the area they were from or struggling to build their own church. I found contacts at churches in Santee, Beaufort, and Georgetown and spoke in many of them, but they looked at the PowerPoint program as an evening of entertainment. There were no serious inquiries or concerns about how the work would continue.

More time passed. I got depressed. I questioned God more. Was there really a plan for somebody else from the United States to help? What would happen if all support was suddenly withdrawn?

Oftentimes I am asked how long do you think it will be before they are financially independent? This is great American thinking, but not in the light of God's economy. I have spoken with several mission groups about this and almost all support for missions comes from the United States. There are some that have resources readily available in country and they can flourish and even give to other countries. For the most part, especially for Third World countries, I have a problem with that question. God does not see congregations from different countries. From God's perspective there is but one church. That church is worldwide. "For God so loved the world."

When Scripture tells us to help the poor in our congregation this encompasses the entire world. There are currently some wealthy church groups in Western Europe and a few other places around the globe, but the majority are in the US. Yes, we should help and encourage people to help themselves, but in many Third World countries they can barely make enough in six days to feed their families a sparse meal. There are families on welfare living in government housing here that have more luxuries than a doctor working in a Mexican government hospital 60+ hours a week. It is incumbent upon those in the family of God who have been given much to help, encourage, and build up those who have little or no resources.

These things crossed my mind as I despaired more and more of the lack of interest for making any sacrifice to help this poor area of Christ's church.

Withdrawing from making new contacts, hoping to hear from someone, anyone, my faith got weaker, my prayers less fervent, and I continued to complain to God. At this time, I began again a study of the life of Abraham. He walked the edge of the desert toward the promised land. He didn't see the promise fulfilled. But he kept walking. And he didn't complain. Only when we move in faith does that faith, now turned to action, becomes a living powerful force in our lives that can and will overcome anything.

I knew the only way out of this funk was to do something. I became more aggressive contacting larger churches with more financial, training, and people resources.

That's when I thought of Pastor Larry Burgbacher of the megachurch Faith Assemblies of God in Summerville. I had had lunches with Larry and my good friend Barney on a couple of occasions and the message had always been received with love and grace. Faith Assembly is extremely mission minded, supporting over 100 missionaries and were faithful to a small financial commitment to Mission Acapulco. I sent an email and received a response the next day to meet.

Barney went with me and before I asked to speak to some of the groups and satellite churches, I vented my frustrations. I expressed my concern for purity of the teaching as the work was scattered and needed cohesiveness in training. Larry looked at Barney and asked him to open up his group and others for me to speak and see what God does.

Before I left the church campus, Barney made arrangements for me to speak to his prayer group. I prayed that no matter how big or small the group that God would provide a new treasurer (our treasurer, who had been faithful to the task for many years, asked to be replaced as well) and perhaps someone to just go to Acapulco to see the work firsthand. I arrived to a group of five.

Barney, sensing my disappointment, waited to start, hoping more would show. Two did. I showed the PowerPoint presentation, then shared the need. After prayer in the presence of the Holy Spirit, two men stepped forward. One said he would love to be the treasurer, he had experience. The other was a retired pastor from South America and was interested in making the visit.

I jumped for joy as I went to my car that evening and headed home. My wife shared my excitement when I told her what God had done. But God's plan was bigger still.

Sometime after I met with these men, I received a call from the one to be treasurer. His wife had difficulties with him doing this and they had other issues needing resolve. I was angry and not very gracious to him (for which I later apologized). When I met the other gentleman for breakfast later that week, he informed me that he felt God had assigned him to another ministry (in which he has been greatly blessed). I was back at the beginning.

I spoke with Barney and he suggested I speak with George Jager, pastor of the Spanish campus of Faith. As a matter fact, he had already arranged a date.

It was a weekday night, their regular prayer meeting night. I was told to expect 20-30 people. Close to 60 arrived. They connected my laptop to a a big screen TV so all could better see. The pastor and his wife, both from Peru, which is a bit different Spanish, were unable to be there because of the flu. In spite of the large turnout, I took their absence as a bad sign.

The presentation went well. I explained the need and that I felt my time of active ministry in Mexico neared the end. Many gave positive remarks and asked how they could help. An offering was taken and a total of $300 was given—remarkable considering the impromptu presentation. I was encouraged, but still wondered what was next.

Soon after, the pastor, touched by the Spirit of God through those who were there, contacted me to arrange a meeting. We discussed the benefits to his church of being affiliated with Mission Acapulco. We talked about how we were able to support ourselves independently and with the donations we regularly received. We reviewed the need for good teaching and oversight and cohesiveness. The Assemblies of God are active all over the world in many cultures and have been able to maintain this cohesiveness and purity of doctrine. We then met with Larry and shared these plans, and he gave the okay to arrange to take a group on a teaching mission and for them to get an overview of the entire ministry.

The leadership in Mexico requested teaching on the role of women in the church, the role of the pastor, and how to make Google messages. I also taught a bit on the book of Revelation and the baptism of the Holy Spirit, two problem topics in the area. The intense five-day schedule gave the group a broad view of the ministry.

We also met with the hierarchy of the Spanish Assemblies of God hoping that they would want to work with us. But I overheard the group (speaking in Spanish not knowing I understood) remarking that they seemed more interested in transferring ownership, including real estate, to the Assemblies of God. This meant transferring pastors to different locations. The group felt this was not in the best interest of Mission Acapulco, especially in the mountains.

On the last day of the trip, Pastor Jager discussed this with the group and how they needed to push ahead with Pastor Burgbacher to take over the work. (He did this in Spanish and English still not realizing I understood.)

I stayed longer to attend the seven-day funeral of the grandmother of one of my Jewish friends. I knew the family well and had many opportunities to discuss the Messiah with them.

Upon returning, George and his wife made a list of those they thought would make good board members. A meeting was called, and a new board voted in. They assured me that I would not be left out of any decision making, though I feel that I need to be quiet and place this ministry in the hands of these people God has chosen, not to be hampered by my vision for its future because God will continue to give them His vision and the ability to carry it out and fulfill the dream and prayer of Captain Reginald Carey Brenton for the people of Southwest Mexico.

Amen. And so be it.

REFERENCES

Boyce, Marguerite P. *Captain Brenton's Heritage: The Gospel Message for Southwest Mexico: Captain Reginald Carey Brenton 1848-1921*. Franklin, Tennessee. Providence House Publishers, 1994

"Acapulco". History of Acapulco. <http://www.acapulco.com/en/general/history.html

www.ingramcontent.com/pod-product-compliance
Lightning Source LLC
Chambersburg PA
CBHW050322120526
44592CB00014B/2010